Blue Line 1

Workbook

Ausgabe für Bayern (Mittelschulen)

Herausgeber: Wolfgang Hamm

Ernst Klett Verlag
Stuttgart • Leipzig

Go on a tour around your book!

Hier könnt ihr ein Spiel spielen, das euch dabei hilft, euer Schulbuch besser kennen zu lernen. Dazu arbeitet ihr in Dreier-Gruppen zusammen und versucht, so schnell wie möglich alle Fragen zu beantworten. Die Lösungen sind im Schulbuch versteckt. Kreist die richtigen Lösungen ein. Wenn ihr fertig seid, sucht euch eine andere Gruppe, die auch fertig ist, und vergleicht eure Lösungen. Wer hat die meisten richtigen Antworten?

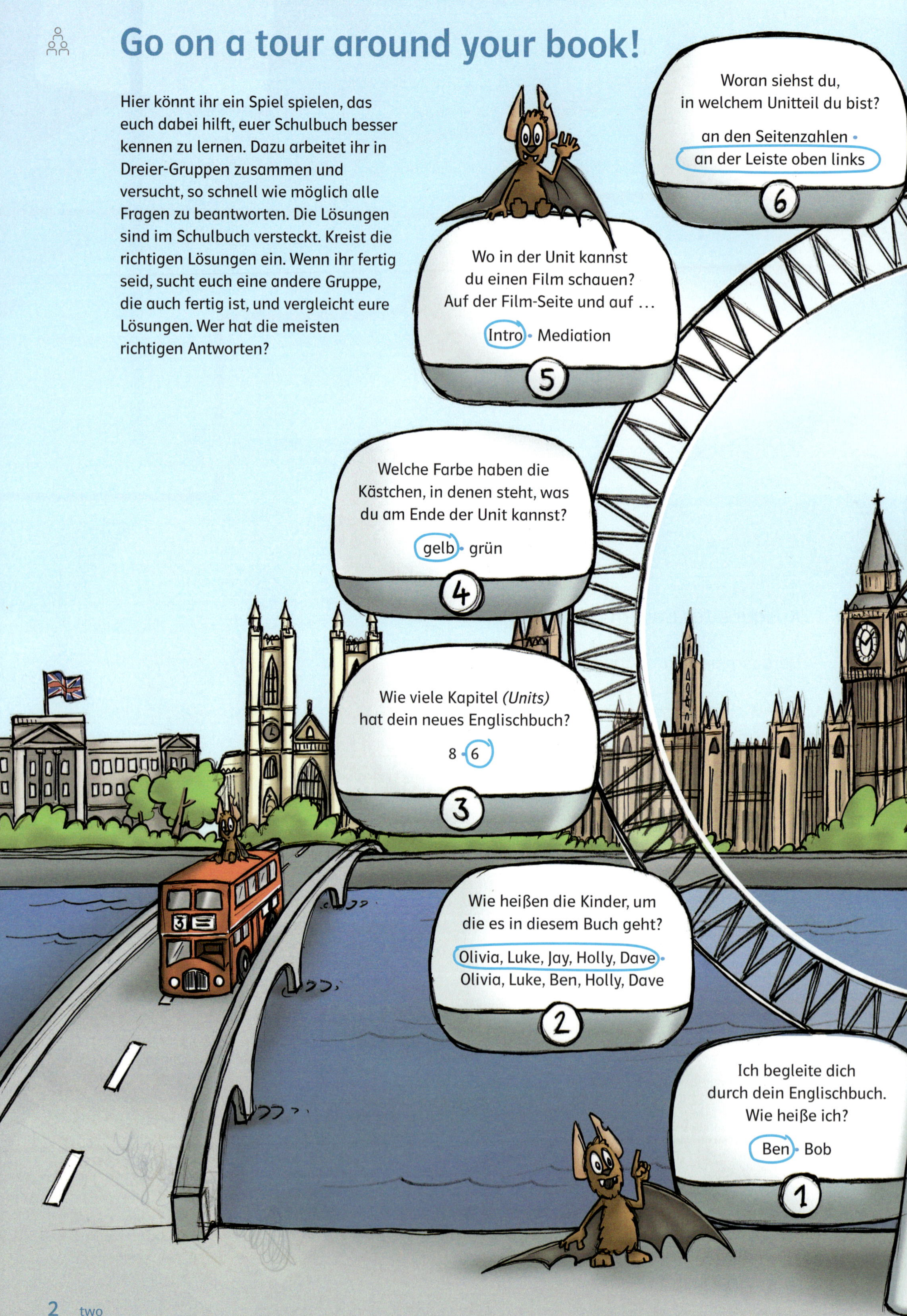

1
Ich begleite dich durch dein Englischbuch. Wie heiße ich?
Ben • Bob
2
Wie heißen die Kinder, um die es in diesem Buch geht?
Olivia, Luke, Jay, Holly, Dave • Olivia, Luke, Ben, Holly, Dave
3
Wie viele Kapitel *(Units)* hat dein neues Englischbuch?
8 • 6
4
Welche Farbe haben die Kästchen, in denen steht, was du am Ende der Unit kannst?
gelb • grün
5
Wo in der Unit kannst du einen Film schauen? Auf der Film-Seite und auf …
Intro • Mediation
6
Woran siehst du, in welchem Unitteil du bist?
an den Seitenzahlen • an der Leiste oben links

Das London Eye ist ein großes Riesenrad und steht an der Themse. Von dort hast du einen tollen Überblick über London. Genauso gewinnst du mit diesem Spiel einen Überblick über dein Schulbuch.

Mein Sprachenpass

Hello! I'm Ben.

Ich möchte dich dieses Jahr beim Englischlernen begleiten und dir helfen, alles gut zu verstehen. Bevor wir anfangen, möchte ich gerne noch etwas von dir erfahren.

What's your name?

My name: ______________________________

My class: ______________________________

My school: ______________________________

(Individuelle Lösung)

Diese Sprachen kenne ich schon: (Individuelle Lösung)

Zu Hause spreche ich: ______________________________

Manche meiner Freunde sprechen zu Hause: ______________________________

Diese Sprachen habe ich schon einmal im Radio, Fernsehen oder im Urlaub gehört:

____

____

So lerne ich gerne Englisch: (Individuelle Lösung)

Setze Häkchen.

- ☐ mit Liedern 
- ☐ durch Zuhören 
- ☐ beim Spielen 
- ☐ am Computer 
- ☐ beim Lesen 
- ☐ im Urlaub 
- ☐ in der Schule 
- ☐ ______________________________

Welcome – Hello!

Hello! I'm Ben the bat!
Nice to meet you. What's
your name? I like English.

8/1 **1** Find the two sentences.

Finde die beiden Sätze heraus und schreibe sie auf.

NICETOMEETYOUILIKEENGLISH

Nice to ______

8/1 **2** Match the sentences.

Ordne den englischen Sätzen ihre deutschen Übersetzungen zu.

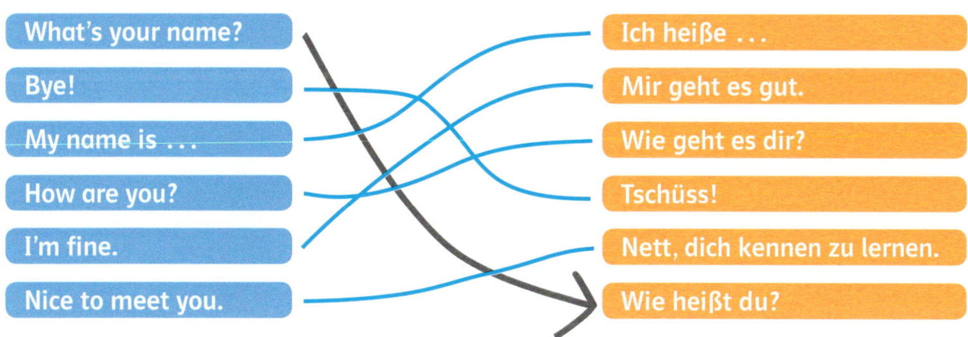

What's your name?
Bye!
My name is …
How are you?
I'm fine.
Nice to meet you.
Ich heiße …
Mir geht es gut.
Wie geht es dir?
Tschüss!
Nett, dich kennen zu lernen.
Wie heißt du?

8/1 **3** Complete the dialogue.

Vervollständige den Dialog.

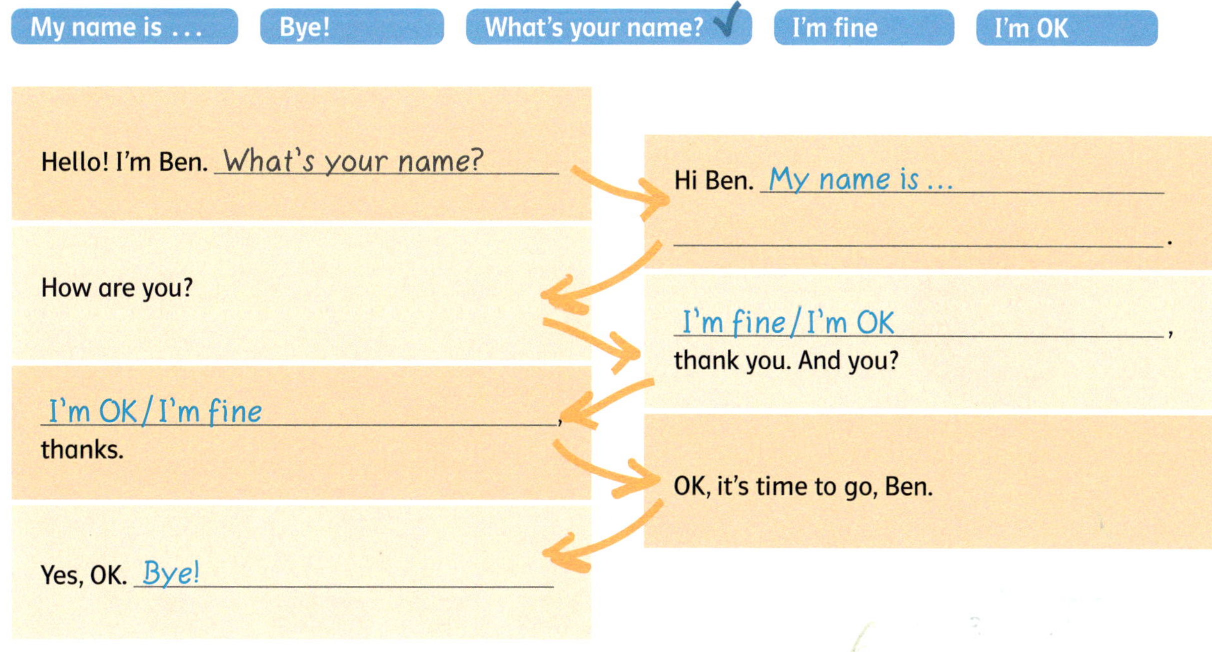

9/2 ## 4 Write the numbers.

Was zeigen die Würfel an? Schreibe die Zahlen.

1. two
2. four
3. five
4. ten
5. three
6. eight

9/2 ## 5 Connect the number words with a blue line.

Verbinde die Zahlenwörter in ihrer richtigen Reihenfolge mit einer blauen Linie.

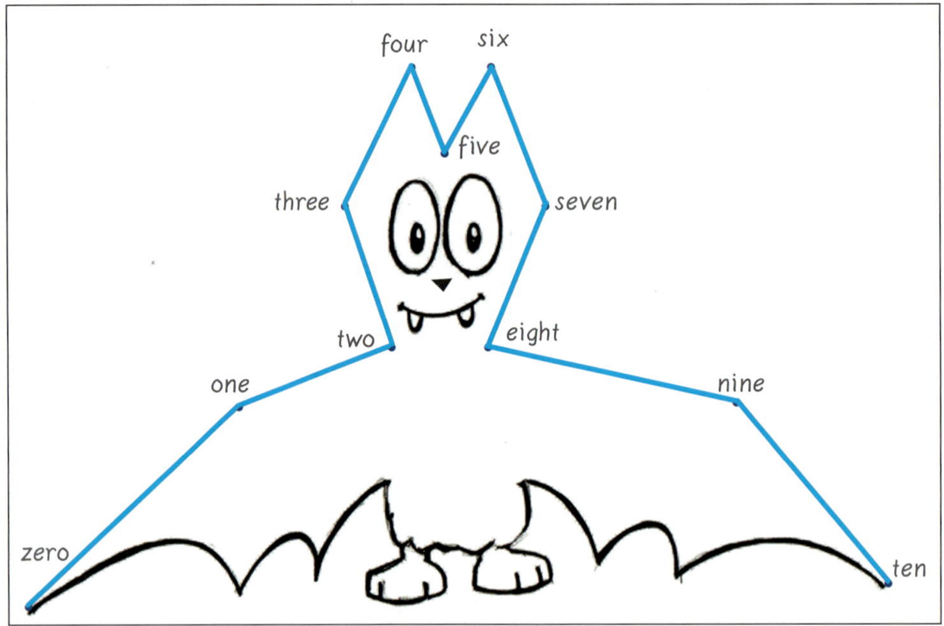

9/2 ## 6 Write your favourite colours. (Individuelle Lösung)

Wähle für jeden Ball eine Lieblingsfarbe. Male die Bälle aus und schreibe die Farbe darunter.

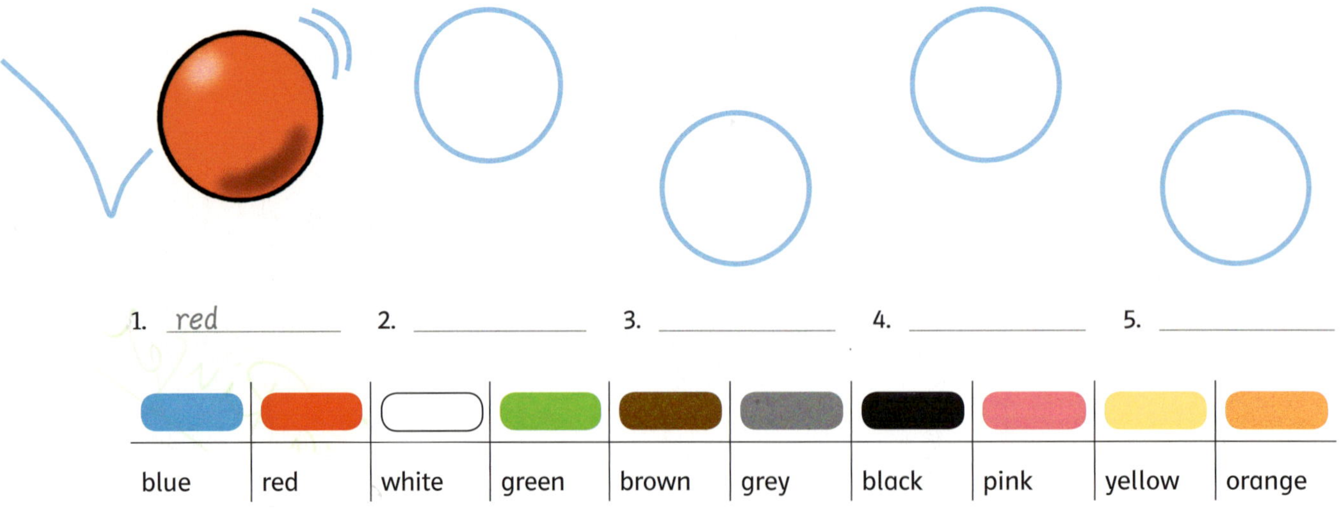

Zoom in – In a park

10/1 ## 1 Cross out the wrong word.

Welches Wort gehört nicht in die Reihe? Streiche es durch.

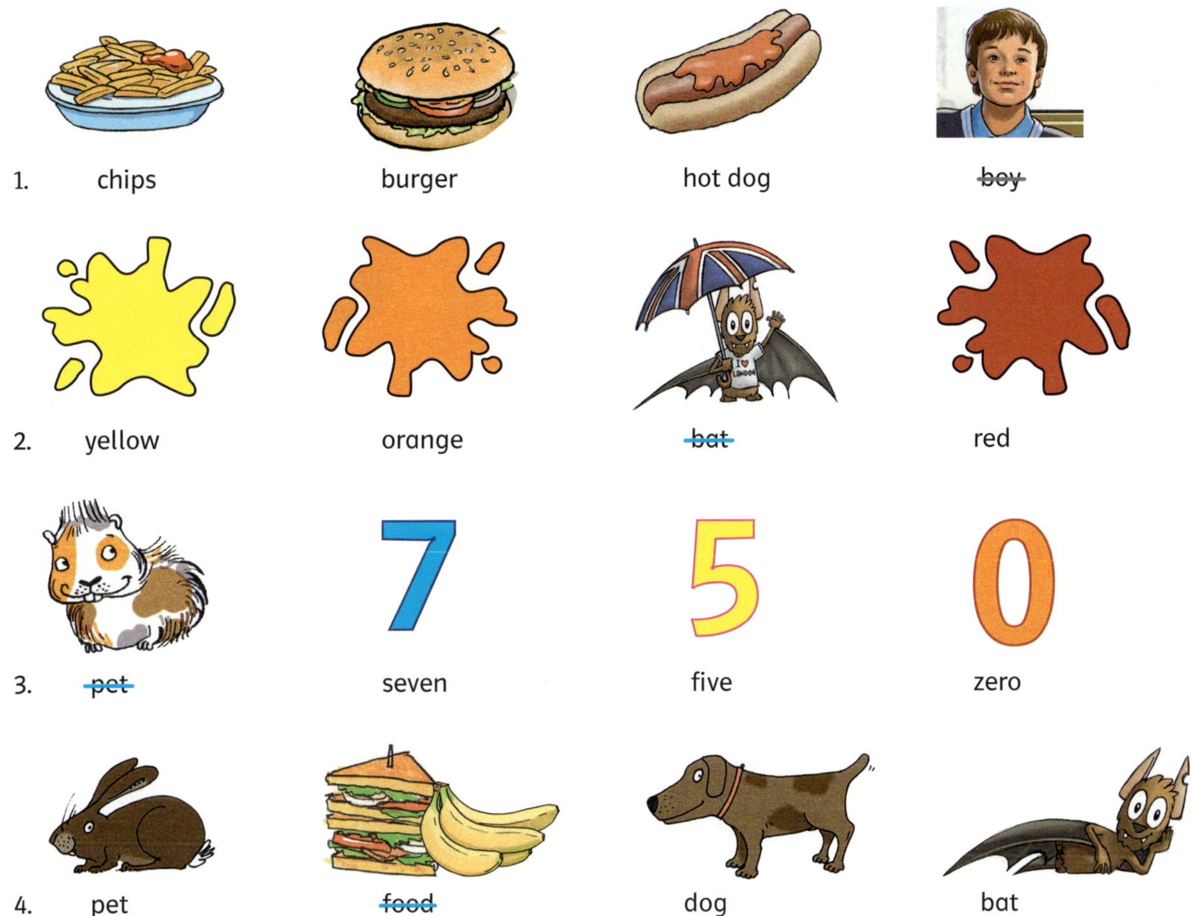

1. chips burger hot dog ~~boy~~
2. yellow orange ~~bat~~ red
3. ~~pet~~ seven five zero
4. pet ~~food~~ dog bat

11/4 ## 2 Write the words.

Schreibe die richtigen Wörter unter die Bilder.

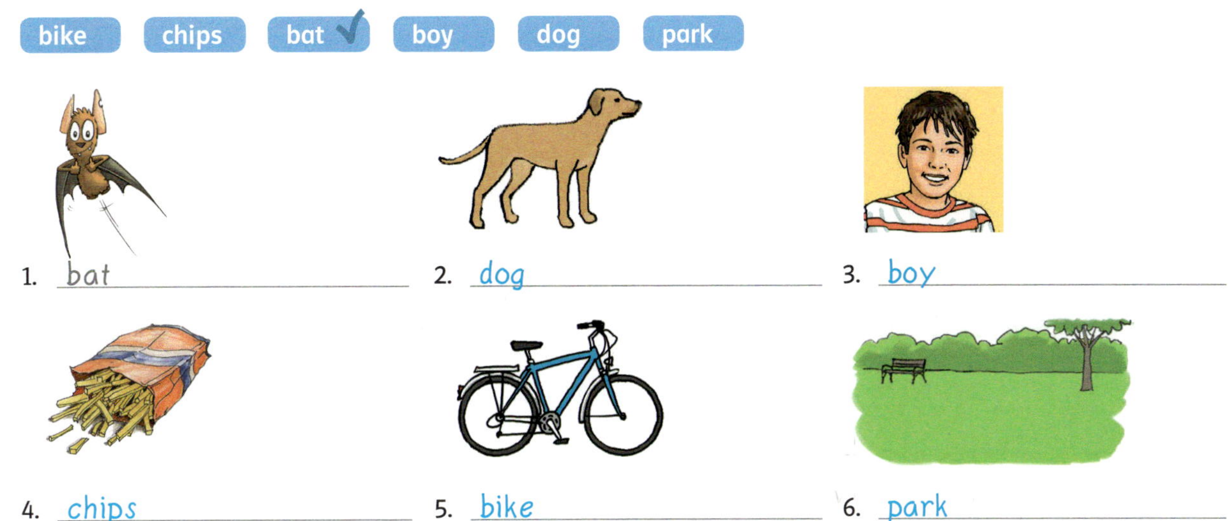

bike | chips | bat ✓ | boy | dog | park

1. bat
2. dog
3. boy
4. chips
5. bike
6. park

I'm from Greenwich

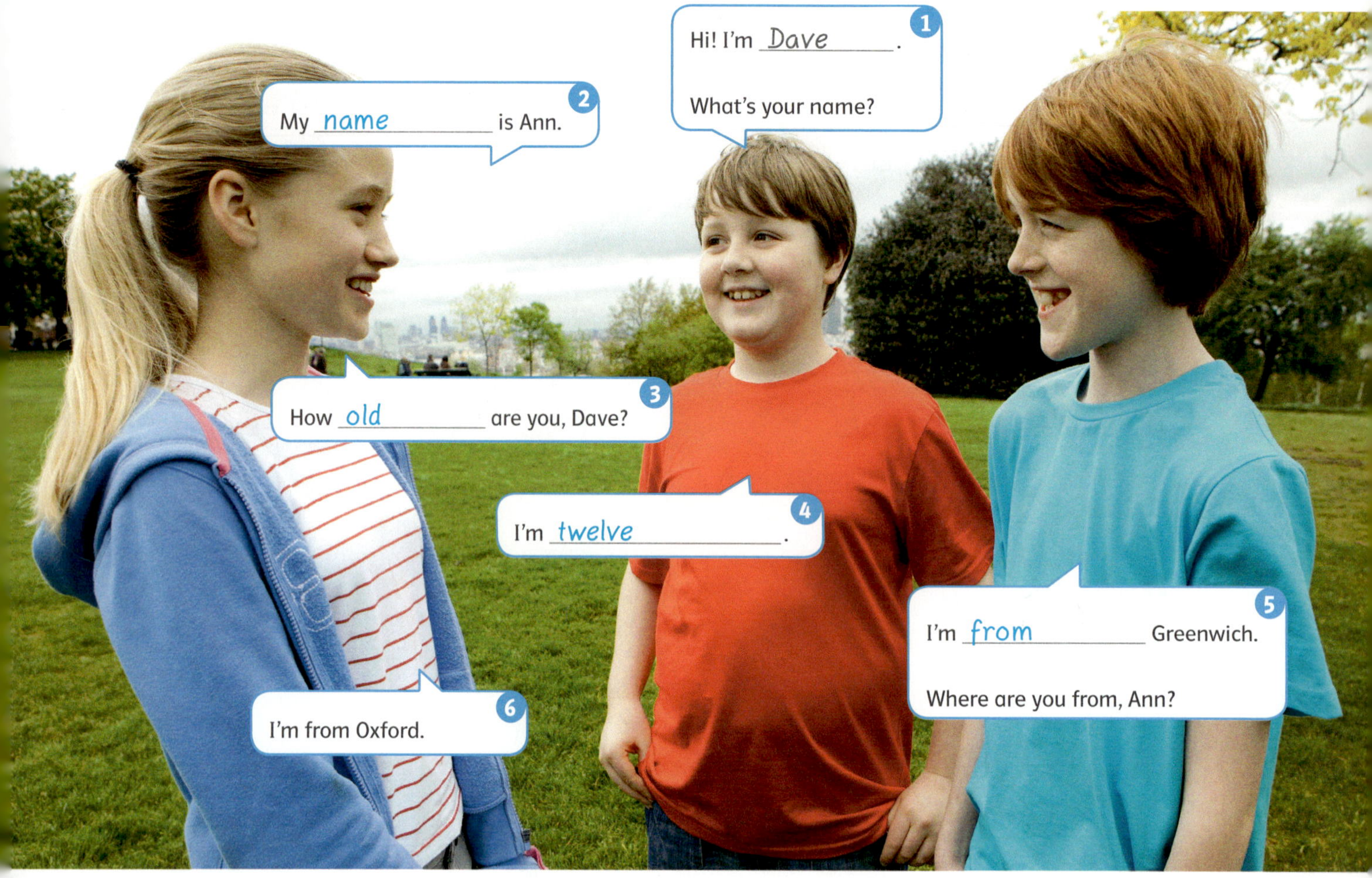

1. Hi! I'm _Dave_____.
   What's your name?
2. My _name_______ is Ann.
3. How _old_______ are you, Dave?
4. I'm _twelve_________.
5. I'm _from_________ Greenwich.
   Where are you from, Ann?
6. I'm from Oxford.

12/2 **1 Put in the right words.**

Setze die richtigen Wörter ein.

from | Dave ✓ | name | old | twelve

13/3 **2 What's your name?**

a) Verbinde die Fragen und Antworten.

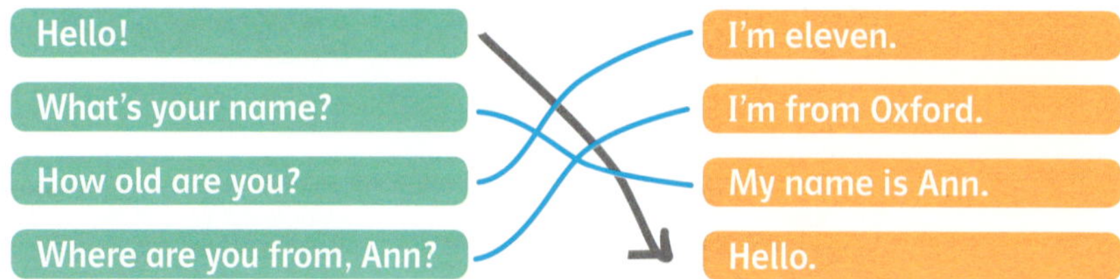

Hello!
What's your name?
How old are you?
Where are you from, Ann?
I'm eleven.
I'm from Oxford.
My name is Ann.
Hello.

b) Gehe im Klassenzimmer herum und suche dir eine Partnerin / einen Partner.
Spielt dann gemeinsam den Dialog aus a) nach.

1 15/4 **1 (SOUNDS) Listen and tick ✓ the words with [ð].**

Höre zu und setze ein Häkchen an die Wörter, bei denen du [ð] hörst.

☑ 

☐ 

☐ 

☑ 

2 (WRITING) Write the family words.

15/5a a) Finde die Wörter und schreibe sie auf.

1. family
2. father
3. mother
4. sister
5. brother
6. friend

15/5b b) Decke nun die Wörter in a) ab und versuche, sie aus dem Gedächtnis aufzuschreiben.

1. family
2. father
3. mother
4. sister
5. brother
6. friend

15/6 **3 Find the right name. Put it in the right form.**

Finde den Namen heraus und setze die richtige Form ein.

1. Sherlock is Luke's dog.

2. Holly's pets are nice.

3. Dave's cat is cool.

4. Lucy is Olivia's sister.

5. Desmond is Lucy's father.

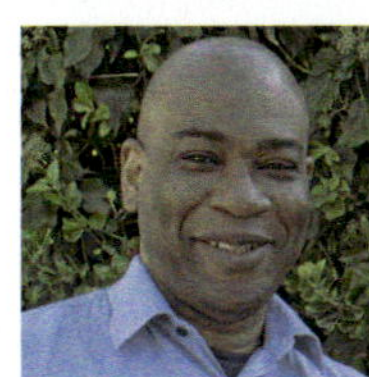

6. Claire is Desmond's friend.

16/8 ↗ **4 Match the words.**

Ordne die Wörter richtig zu.

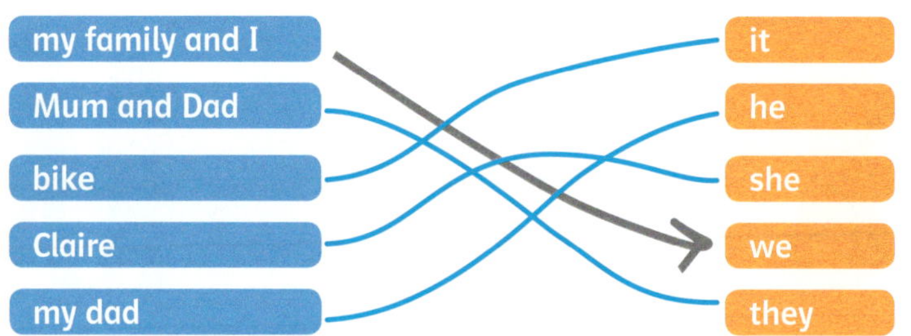

5 Look at Claire's family photos.

16/9 ↗ **a)** Wähle das richtige Wort. Kreise es ein.

1. Desmond and Lucy are / is in the garden.
2. I am / are with Lucy.
3. Janet are / is Olivia's mum.
4. Desmond am / is in the garden.
5. Olivia and her mum is / are in the park.

16/10a ↗ **b)** Setze am, is oder are ein.

This is ________ a nice photo of the Fraser family. I am ________ Lucy's mum. We are ________ in Desmond's garden. Olivia is ________ eleven and Lucy is five. Olivia's mum is ________ nice.

17/11 ## 6 Complete the chart.

Ergänze die Tabelle.

long form	short form
I am	I'm
you are	you're
he is	he's
she is	she's
it is	it's
we are	we're
they are	they're

17/11 ## 7 Put in short forms.

Setze die Kurzformen ein.

he's it's I'm ✓ he's I'm

Hello, Sid here. Yes, I'm Dave's cat.

Dave? He's twelve. Yes, I'm his friend.

Dave's bike? It's cool!

Luke's dog? He's black and white!

17/13 ## 8 Find the names for the family tree.

1. Karen and Bill are Nancy's mother and father.
2. Harry is Nancy's brother.
3. Helen is Nancy's sister.

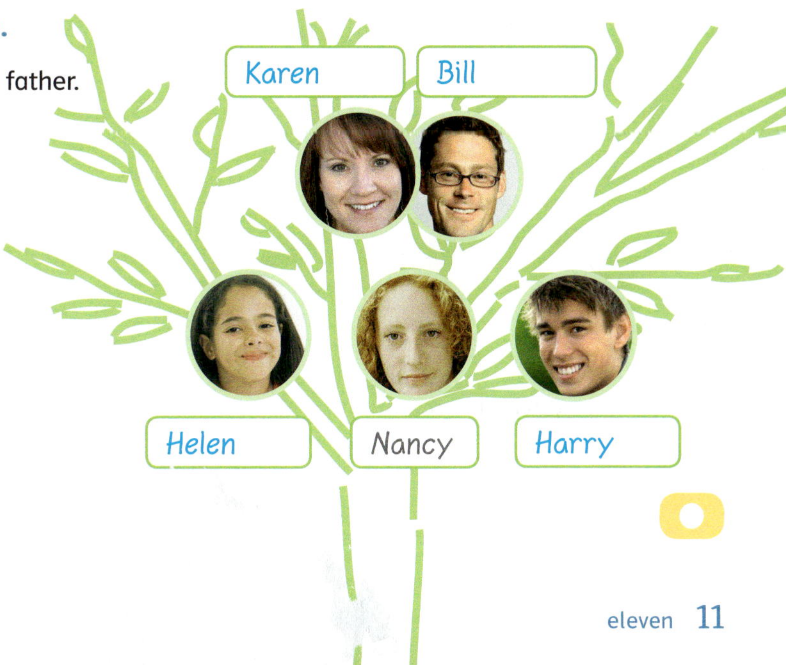

18/2 1 Write the words.

Schreibe die Wörter.

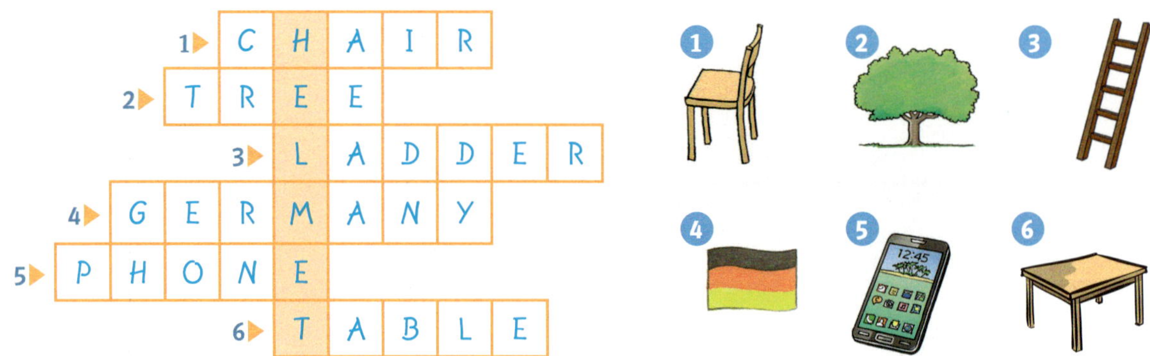

Wie lautet das Lösungswort? Schreibe es auf. helmet

18/4 2 Look at the pictures and put in the right words.

Schau dir die Bilder an und setze die richtigen Wörter ein.

on | in | under | next to | behind

1. Sid is on the chair.
2. The chair is on the table.
3. Sid is under the books.
4. The box is next to the table.
5. Ben is behind the box.
6. The teddy is in the box.
7. Sid is on the books.
8. The books are under Sid.
9. One book is on the table.
10. The chair is behind the table.
11. The teddy is next to the box.
12. Ben is in the box.

19/6 ↗ **3** **Look, count and write.**

Schau genau und zähle nach, wie oft sich die Gegenstände auf diesem Bild befinden. Schreibe auf.

2 helmets
3 ladders
5 chairs
2 tables
3 balls
4 books
2 teddies
2 boxes

Achte auf Wörter, die auf -x oder -y enden:
box – box**es**
family – famil**ies**

20/9 ↗ **4** **Put in There's or There are.**

a) Setze There's oder There are ein.

1. There are two trees.
2. There's a ladder under one tree.
3. There's a table next to the trees.
4. There are three chairs behind the table.
5. Oh no! There's a cat in the tree.

b) Setze There's oder There are ein. Zeichne die Gegenstände ins Bild und male es an.

1. There's a box under the table.
2. There are two balls. They're in the box.
3. There's a teddy on the table.
4. There are two books next to the table.
5. There's a dog next to the tree.

2 21/2 **1** (LISTENING) **Listen and complete the words.**

Höre zu und vervollständige die Wörter.

a e i o u

1. fl a t
2. h o u s e
3. g a rd e n
4. b a lc o ny
5. c o l o u r
6. m e ss
7. r e a dy
8. n e i ghb o u r
9. h o m e

22/3 **2** **Make questions. Use is or are.**

Bilde Fragen. Verwende is oder are.

1. Are you from Germany?
2. Are you ten?
3. Is your mobile black?
4. Is your pet a dog?
5. Are Olivia and Holly sisters?
6. Is Dave from Greenwich?

23/7 **3** **Make questions. Put in who, where or what.**

Bilde Fragen. Setze who, where oder what ein.

1. What 's this? – It's a phone.

Vorsicht!

Who? Wer?
Where? Wo?

2. Where 's Ben? – He's in a box.

3. Who 's he? – He's Luke.

4. And who 's she? – She's Olivia.

5. What 's this? – It's a bag.

6. Where 's Sid? – He's under the chair.

7. Who 's Sid? – He's Dave's cat.

24/4 ↗ **1** (READING) **What's in the story? Tick ✓ the right things and people.**

Was steht in der Geschichte? Setze ein Häkchen an die richtigen Gegenstände und Leute.

24/4 ↗ **2** (READING) **Match the sentence parts.**

Verbinde die Satzteile.

1. Olivia and her dad
2. Olivia is
3. There's wood
4. Lucy is
5. Holly is on
6. There's

a. and there's a ladder.
b. in the new tree house.
c. are in the garden.
d. the ladder.
e. a funny noise.
f. there too.

26/2 ↗ **3** (MEDIATION) **Stelle Sue vor.** (Individuelle Lösung)

Du musst dabei nicht Wort für Wort übersetzen. Gib nur die wichtigsten Informationen weiter.

Das ist ....
Sie ist ... alt. Ihr ....
Sie kommt aus ....
Sie ist ein ....
Sie möchte gerne wissen, ...

Hello!

My name is Sue Miller.
That's really Susan.
I'm 11. My birthday is in November.
I'm from Liverpool. It's in the north of England. Liverpool is nice.
This is a photo of it.
I like ☺ football. I'm a fan of Manchester United.

And what about you? Where are you from? And how old are you?

Lösungen online
zu9h8f

1. Löse alle Aufgaben.
2. Überprüfe deine Lösungen online. Gib dazu Bens Code in das Suchfeld auf der Klett-Homepage ein. (Die Internetadresse findest du ganz vorne im Heft in der Legende.)
3. Gib dir selbst Punkte. Wenn du weniger als die Hälfte der Punkte hast, male das Kästchen rot aus und übe auf den Step by step-Seiten (z. B. bei Unit 1 auf S. 18–19).

___/5P

Ziel 1: Ich kann mich vorstellen.

→ p. 18/1

Look at Linda's poster. What can she say?
Schau dir Lindas Poster an. Was kann sie sagen?

Hi! My name is Linda. I'm Steve's sister.

I'm from London. That's in England.

I'm a football fan. Football is cool.

___/6P

Ziel 2: Ich kann über meine Familie sprechen.

→ p. 18/2

Put in the right words.
Setze die richtigen Wörter ein.

This is my family.

Kate and Rob are my mum and dad.

Max and Steve are my brothers.

Fay is my sister. Our pets

are here too. Two cats and one dog.

___/5P

Ziel 3: Ich kann sagen, wo sich etwas befindet.

→ p. 18/3

Look at the picture and complete the sentences.
Sieh dir das Bild an und vervollständige die Sätze.

1. A box is on the table.
2. Ben is in the box.
3. A helmet is next to the table.
4. A football is under the table.
5. A ladder is behind the table.

___/4P Ziel 4: Ich kann mich über mein Zuhause unterhalten.

→p. 19/4

Answer the questions. Beantworte die Fragen.

flat | balcony | neighbours | at home

1. Where's Holly? She's at home.
2. Is Holly's home a flat or a house? It's a flat.
3. Is there a balcony or a garden? There's a balcony.
4. Who's in the flat next to Holly's flat? There are her neighbours.

___/3P Ziel 5: Ich kann eine Bildergeschichte verstehen.

→p. 19/5

Match the sentences with the pictures. Ordne den Bildern die richtigen Sätze zu.

The garden is a mess. 4

The garden is nice. A cat is on the table. 1

Sherlock! No! 3

There's a noise. 2

___/4P Ziel 6: Ich kann zwei Personen miteinander bekannt machen.

→p. 19/6

Hello! My name is Steve. I'm from Liverpool. Where are you from?
I have a brother. And you?
Das ist …
Hallo! Ich heiße Jana. Ich komme aus Stuttgart.
Ich habe eine Schwester.

Jana möchte Steve kennen lernen. Stell ihn vor.

Das ist Steve. Er kommt aus Liverpool.

Er fragt: Woher kommst du?

Er hat einen Bruder.

Er möchte wissen: Hast du Geschwister?

Lösungen online
zu9h8f

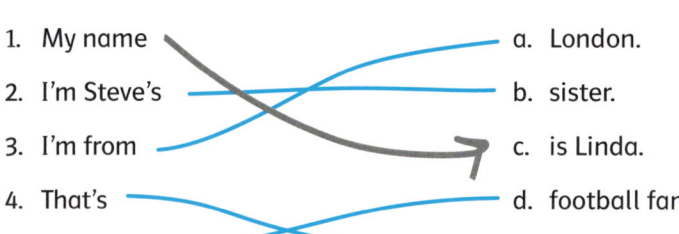

Ziel 1: Ich kann mich vorstellen.

○ **a)** Lies dir alle Satzteile durch und verbinde dann die Satzteile, die zusammengehören.

1. My name	a. London.
2. I'm Steve's	b. sister.
3. I'm from	c. is Linda.
4. That's	d. football fan.
5. I'm a	e. in England.

○ **b)** Fülle die Lücken mit Informationen über dich aus. (Individuelle Lösung)

Hello! My name is ______________________.

I'm from ______________________.

That's in ______________________.

○ Ziel 2: Ich kann über meine Familie sprechen.

Was erzählt Lucy über ihre Familie? Setze die richtigen Wörter ein.

father | brothers | sister | family ✓ | mother

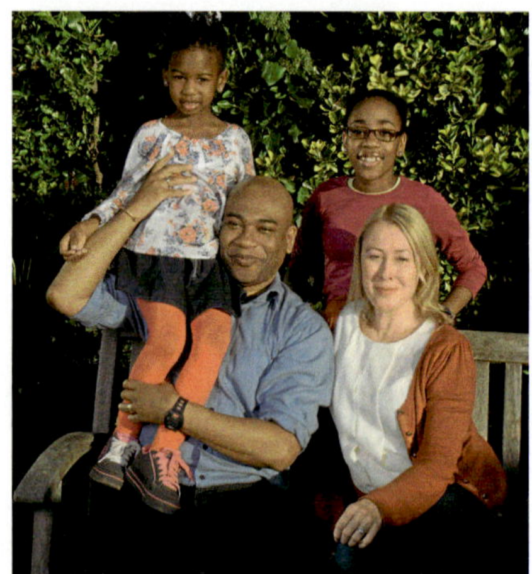

1. Hello! My name is Lucy. I'm five and this is my family.
2. Here's Olivia. She's my sister.
3. I have no brothers.
4. This is Desmond. He's our father.
5. Claire is my mother. She's nice.

○ Ziel 3: Ich kann sagen, wo sich etwas befindet.

Setze die richtigen Wörter ein.

1. A box is on the chair.
2. Ben is in the box.
3. A ladder is next to the chair.
4. A football is under the chair.
5. A helmet is behind the ladder.

Ziel 4: Ich kann mich über mein Zuhause unterhalten.

Beantworte die Fragen. Kreise die richtige Lösung ein.

1. Where's Holly? — She's at home / in the garden.
2. Is Holly's home a flat or a house? — It's a house / a flat.
3. Is there a balcony or a garden? — There's a balcony / a garden.
4. Who's in the flat next to Holly's flat? — There are her neighbours / pets.
5. What's that next to Olivia? — It's a bike / a balcony.

Ziel 5: Ich kann eine Bildergeschichte verstehen.

Bringe die Bilder in die richtige Reihenfolge. Schreibe die Zahlen 1–4 in die Kästchen.

3 Sherlock! No!

4 The garden is a mess.

1 The garden is nice. A cat is on the table.

2 There's a noise.

Ziel 6: Ich kann zwei Personen miteinander bekannt machen.

Welche Sätze enthalten die gleiche Information? Verbinde sie.

1. Hello! My name is Steve.
2. I'm from Liverpool.
3. Where are you from?
4. I have a brother.
5. How old are you?

a. Er kommt aus Liverpool.
b. Er hat einen Bruder.
c. Er fragt, wie alt du bist.
d. Er fragt, woher du kommst.
e. Das ist Steve.

Merke dir die Sätze. Wenn du zwei Personen miteinander bekannt machen willst, wirst du sie immer wieder brauchen.

This is my school

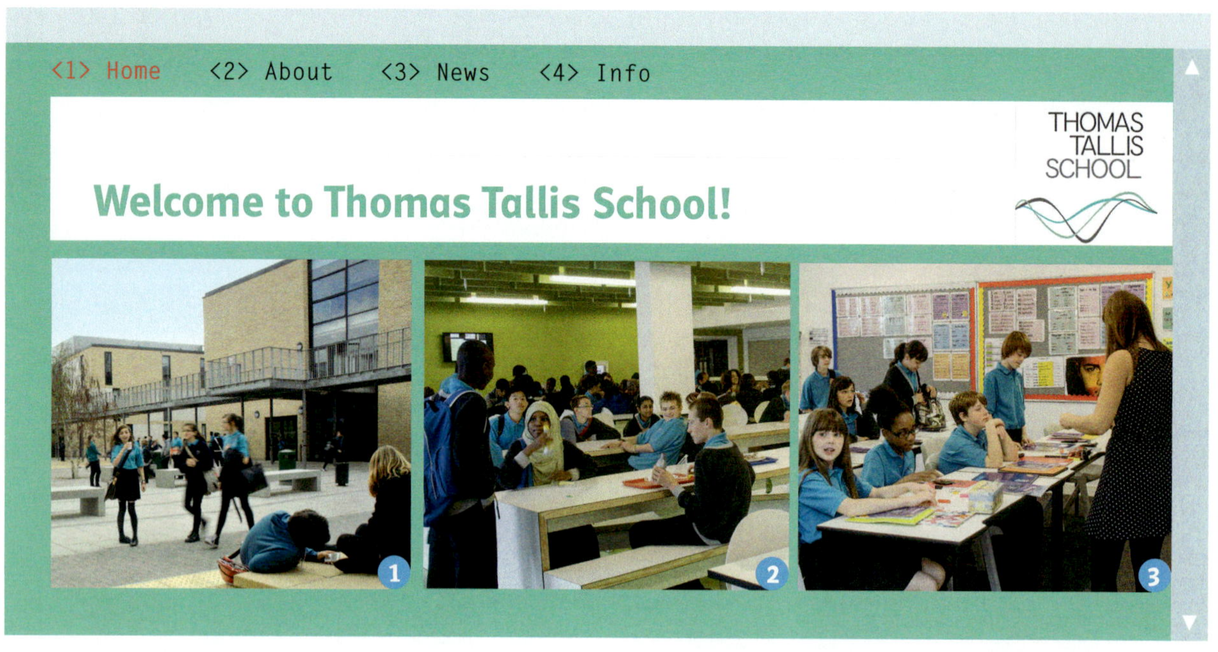

30/1 **1** **Put in the right words.**

cafeteria | eat | play | playground ✓ | teacher | classroom

1. You can play games in the playground.
2. You can eat food in the cafeteria.
3. Mrs Bond is in the classroom. She's an English teacher.

30/2 **2** **Complete the mind map.**

Vervollständige die Mindmap.

classroom ✓ | talk to friends | playground | teacher | caretaker | cafeteria | student | eat food | play games

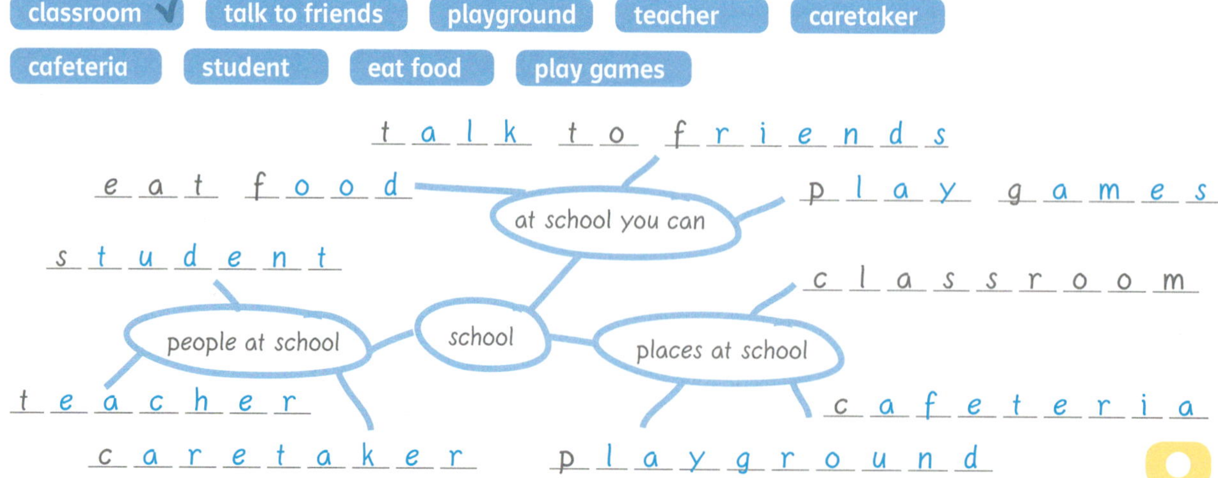

33/4 ↗ **1** Match the pictures with the right words.

a) Ordne den Bildern die richtigen Wörter zu.

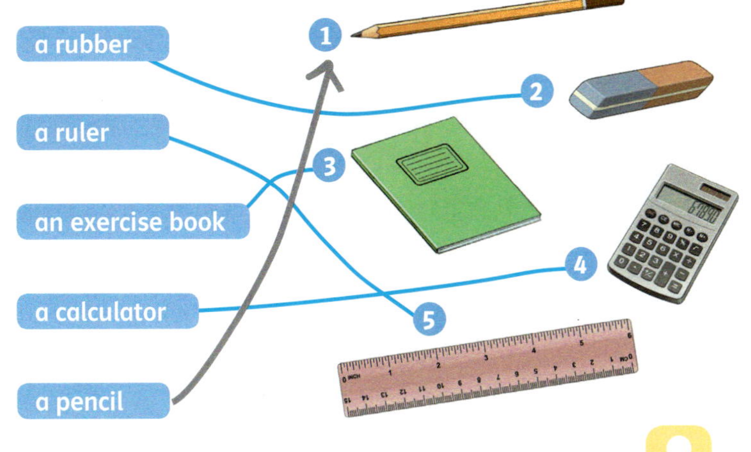

b) Schreibe die Wörter.

1. a pencil
2. (a) rubber
3. (an) exercise book
4. (a) calculator
5. (a) ruler

33/4 ↗ **2** Put in a, an or the.

a) Setze a oder an ein.

1. a bag an orange bag
2. a teacher an English teacher
3. an exercise a new exercise
4. an answer a good answer

b) Setze a, an oder the ein.

1. Mrs Bond is an English teacher.
2. There's a book in her bag.
3. The book in her bag is blue.
4. Luke is a football fan.
5. His favourite place is the playground.
6. There's an orange ladder. It's Mrs Warren's ladder.

3
33/5 ↗ **3** (LISTENING) Listen to Dave and Luke. Tick ✓ the things in Dave's bag.

Höre Dave und Luke zu. Kreuze die Dinge in Daves Tasche an.

34/8 4 Match the sentences with the pictures.

Ordne den Bildern die richtigen Sätze zu.

- Don't play games here.
- Listen to the music.
- Eat in the cafeteria, please.
- Don't open the window. ✓
- Don't sit down.

1

Don't open the window.

2

Eat in the cafeteria, please.

3

Don't sit down.

4

Don't play games here.

5
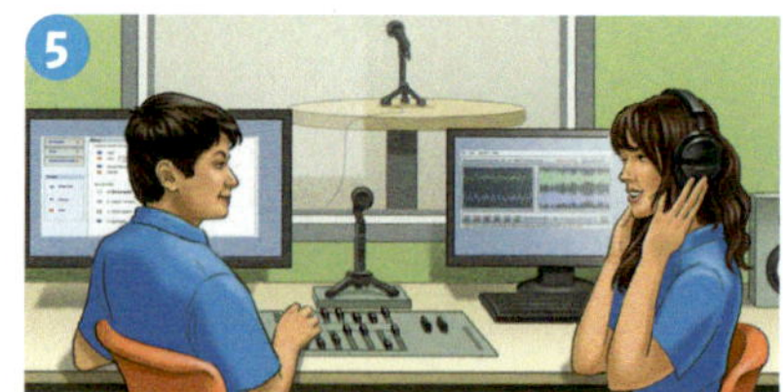

Listen to the music.

35/9 5 Make sentences.

a) Verbinde die passenden Satzteile.

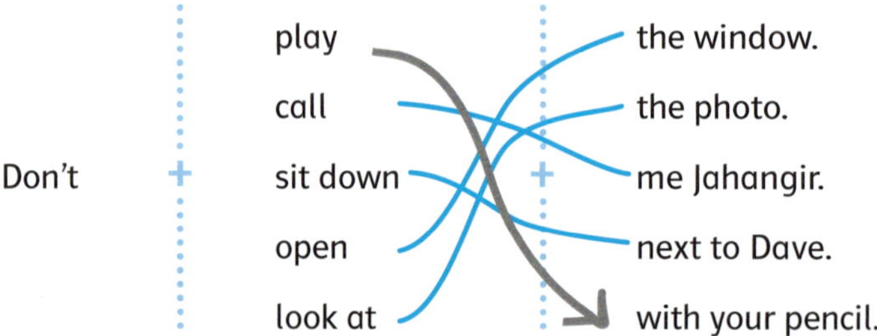

b) Schreibe die Sätze in dein Heft.

35/10 6 (SPEAKING) Tell your partner. (Individuelle Lösung)

a) Gebt euch gegenseitig Anweisungen und führt diese aus.

Example:
Partner A: Open the window, please.
Partner B: Sit on the table.

Partner A: open the window ✓ | look at the book | do exercise 1

Partner B: sit on the table ✓ | talk to a student | close your book | play football

b) Findet weitere Anweisungen und führt diese aus.

36/2 ↗ **1** **Find eight school subjects and write them.**

a) Finde die Schulfächer (→ and ↓).

E	B	I	O	L	O	G	Y	I	E
S	P	H	Y	S	I	C	A	L	D
A	E	S	U	P	S	T	M	O	U
D	T	E	G	E	R	M	A	N	C
E	T	D	E	I	T	U	T	E	A
S	E	N	G	L	I	S	H	F	T
I	N	O	E	T	N	I	S	A	I
G	A	R	T	A	U	C	I	C	O
N	T	I	R	B	N	O	L	H	N
T	E	C	H	N	O	L	O	G	Y

b) Schreibe die gefundenen Schulfächer auf.

Biology, German, Art, PE (Physical Education)

English, Music, Maths, DT (Design Technology)

36/3 ↗ **2** **Find the days of the week.**

a) Finde die Wochentage in der Wortschlange.

SATURDAY/TUESDAY/MONDAY/THURSDAY/SUNDAY/FRIDAY/WEDNESDAY

4 b) Sage die Wochentage in der richtigen Reihenfolge auf: Monday, T…
Die Lösung kannst du dir auf der CD anhören.

5
37/6 ↗ **3** (LISTENING) **Listen. What's Olivia's favourite school day?**

Welcher Tag ist Olivias liebster Schultag? Höre zu und schreibe den richtigen Tag auf.

School timetable

	MON	TUE	WED	THU	FRI
Registration					
Lesson 1	Maths	DT	Maths	German	English
Lesson 2	Art	Maths	PE	Biology	Music
Break					
Lesson 3	English	German	Biology	Maths	Maths

Olivia's favourite day is Monday.

4 Spell your favourite subjects. (Individuelle Lösung)

37/9

Schreibe deine Lieblingsfächer auf. Dann buchstabiere sie deinem Partner / deiner Partnerin.

5 Put in the right words.

38/10

Setze die richtigen Wörter ein.

1. Luke isn't my brother. — is / isn't
2. I'm Luke's friend. — I'm / I'm not
3. I'm not good at German. It's not easy. — I'm / I'm not
4. Sherlock isn't my pet. — is / isn't
5. Sid is my pet. I like cats. — is / isn't

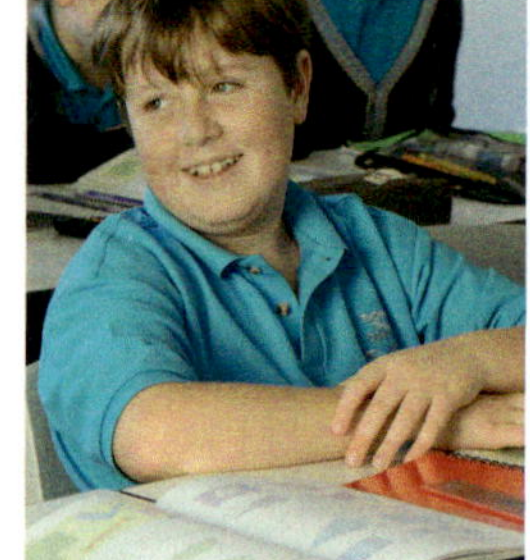

6 (WRITING) Write sentences about Jay and Dave.

38/11

Schreibe Sätze über Jay und Dave.

1. good at computer games • a good singer

2. good at Maths • good at Art

3 x 4 = 12

3. from Germany • from England

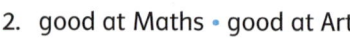

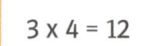

4. in the playground • in the classroom

1. Dave is good at computer games.
   He isn't a good singer.
2. Dave is good at Maths.
   He isn't good at Art.
3. Jay and Dave aren't from Germany.
   They are from England.
4. Jay and Dave are in the playground.
   They aren't in the classroom.

7 (GAME) Play the game. (Individuelle Lösung)

39/14

Je nachdem welche Augenzahl du würfelst, musst du einen englischen Satz mit einem der zwei angegebenen Satzanfängen sagen. Für das Satzende kannst du aus den grünen Wörtern auswählen oder deine eigenen Ideen verwenden.

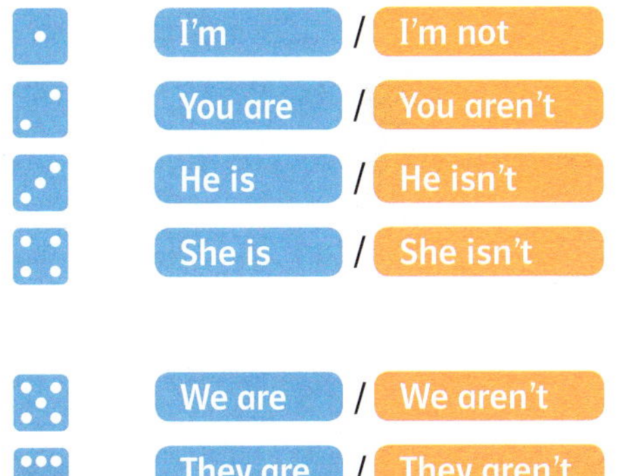

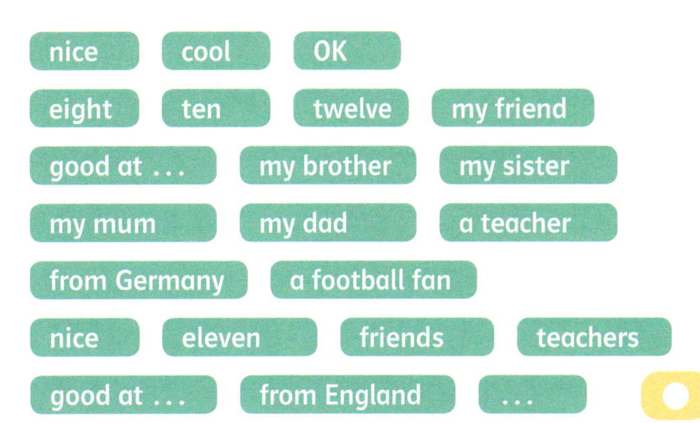

8 That's me. Answer the questions. (Individuelle Lösung)

40/15

a) Klebe ein Bild von dir ein oder zeichne dich. Beantworte die Fragen mit „Yes, I am." oder „No, I'm not.".

b) Wenn du mit „No, I'm not." antwortest, kannst du die Lösung als Antwort mit aufschreiben.

Beispiel:
Are you good at Maths? – No I'm not. I'm good at PE.

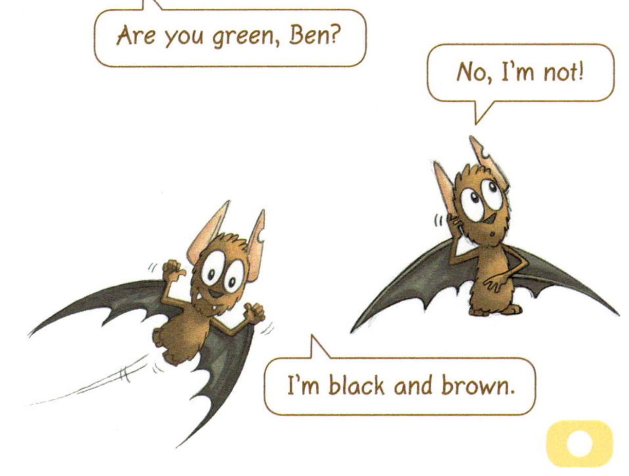

1. Are you a girl? ______
2. Are you eleven? ______
3. Are you good at PE? ______
4. Are you good at English? ______
5. Are you a good singer? ______
6. Are you a football fan? ______

40/16 9 Tell us more about you. (Individuelle Lösung)

Erzähle mehr von dir. Wähle von den Bildern sechs aus. Schreibe sechs Fragen mit Kurzantworten.

1

Are you good at sport?

2

Is this your uniform?

3

Is Art your favourite subject?

4
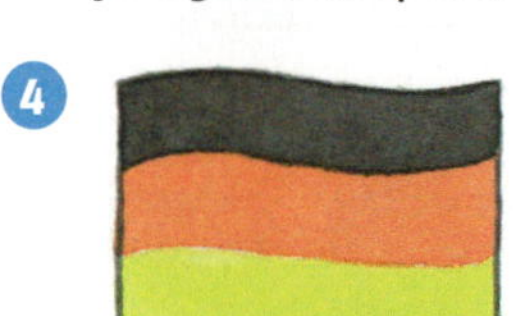
Are you from Germany?

5

Are you in the classroom?

6

Is Saturday your favourite day?

7
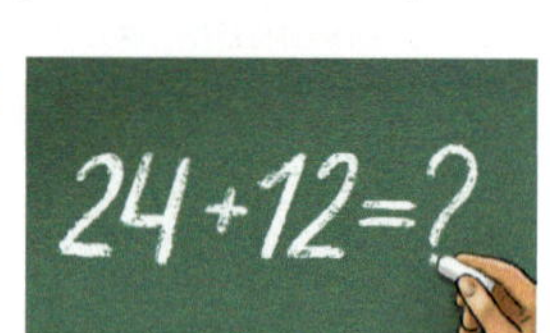

Is Maths easy?

8

Are your teachers nice?

9

Are you a good skater?

1. Are you good at sport? Yes, I am. / No, I'm not.
2. Is this your uniform? No, it …
3. ______
4. ______
5. ______
6. ______

6 41/17 10 (LISTENING) Listen to the Thomas Tallis school radio and tick ✓ the right box.

a) Richtig oder falsch? Höre zu und setze Häkchen.

	right	wrong
1. Jay is a new student at TTS.	✓	☐
2. Olivia is a good singer.	☐	✓
3. Boris isn't a music fan.	☐	✓
4. Luke is good at football.	✓	☐
5. Olivia isn't a football fan.	✓	☐
6. There's a talent show this week.	☐	✓

● b) An welchen Tagen spielt Luke Fußball? Setze Häkchen.

Monday	Tuesday	Wednesday	Thursday	Friday	Saturday	Sunday
✓	☐	✓	☐	☐	✓	☐

42/1 1 (MEDIATION) Gib die Informationen der TTS-Website wieder.

Lies den Veranstaltungshinweis auf der TTS-Website. Setze bei den richtigen Sätzen Häkchen.

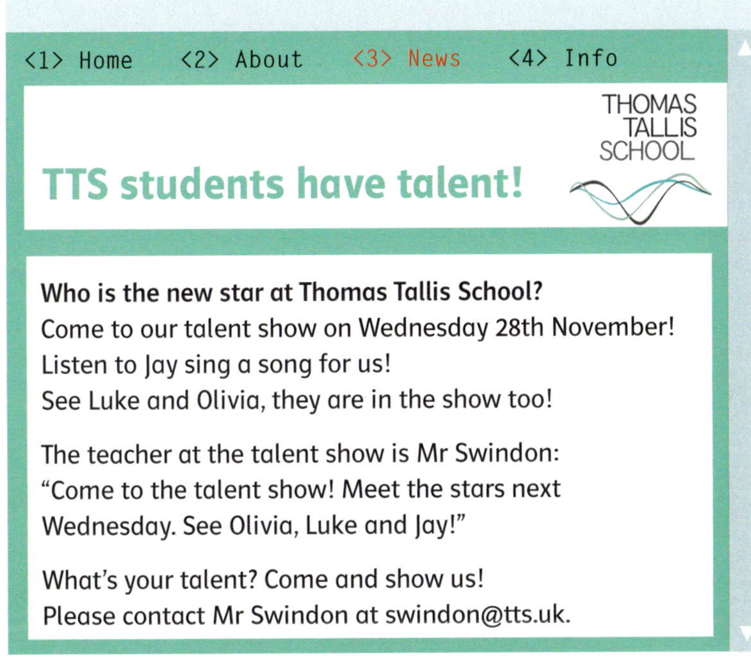

<1> Home <2> About <3> News <4> Info

THOMAS TALLIS SCHOOL

TTS students have talent!

Who is the new star at Thomas Tallis School?
Come to our talent show on Wednesday 28th November!
Listen to Jay sing a song for us!
See Luke and Olivia, they are in the show too!

The teacher at the talent show is Mr Swindon:
"Come to the talent show! Meet the stars next Wednesday. See Olivia, Luke and Jay!"

What's your talent? Come and show us!
Please contact Mr Swindon at swindon@tts.uk.

1. Die Thomas Tallis Schule sucht Kinder, die etwas besonders gut können und zeigen möchten. ☑ ✓
2. Der Talentwettbewerb findet nächsten Donnerstag statt. ☐
3. Jay singt zwei Lieder. ☐
4. Luke und Dave treten ebenfalls auf. ☐
5. Mr Swindon fordert alle auf, nächsten Mittwoch zum Talentwettbewerb zu kommen. ☑ ✓
6. Wenn man am Talentwettbewerb teilnehmen möchte, kann man sich bei Mr Swindon bewerben. ☑ ✓

43/3 2 (READING) Match the sentences with the pictures.

Ordne den Bildern die richtigen Sätze zu.

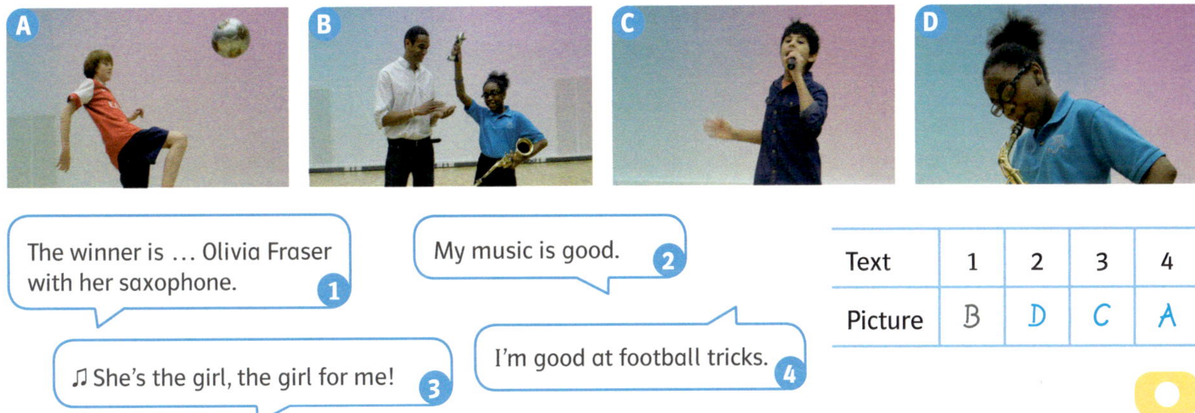
A
B
C
D
The winner is … Olivia Fraser with her saxophone. 1
My music is good. 2
♫ She's the girl, the girl for me! 3
I'm good at football tricks. 4

Text	1	2	3	4
Picture	B	D	C	A

43/3 3 (READING) Complete the sentences.

Vervollständige die Sätze.

1. The friends eat lunch in the cafeteria.
2. Luke's football tricks are cool.
3. Olivia can play the saxophone.
4. Olivia is the winner of the talent show.

lunch ✓ | Olivia | play | football

Lösungen online
9a4d9y

___ /5P

Ziel 1: Ich kann über meine Schule sprechen.

→ p. 30/1

Write sentences about your school. Schreibe Sätze über deine Schule.

Year | classrooms | cafeteria | playground ✓ | eat | play

There's a playground at my school. We can play games and talk there.

There are classrooms too. I'm in Year 5.

My favourite place is the cafeteria. We can eat there. I like the food.

___ /6P

Ziel 2: Ich kann Aufforderungen im Klassenzimmer verstehen und äußern.

→ p. 30/2

a) Match the sentences with the numbers in the pictures.
Welcher Satz passt zu welcher Nummer im Bild? Schreibe die richtige Ziffer neben die Sätze.

Close the window, please. [3] Look at my new phone. [1] Don't talk, please. [2]

b) Oh, here's Mrs Brown. What can she say? Write three sentences.
Oh, hier kommt Frau Brown. Wie kann sie die Kinder zurechtweisen? Schreibe drei Sätze.

1. Listen to the students.
2. Don't sing, please.
3. Sit down, please.

Listen to the students. | Don't eat here. | Don't sing, please. | Sit down, please.

___ /7P

Ziel 3: Ich kann über meinen Schulalltag sprechen.

→ p. 30/3

Write the days of the week and the school subjects. Schreibe die Wochentage und die Schulfächer.

School timetable

	Monday	Tuesday	Wednesday	Thursday	Friday
1	Biology	Music	Biology	German	PE
2	Maths	English	Maths	DT	Art

___ /3P

Ziel 4: Ich kann auf Fragen kurz antworten.

→ p. 31/4

Answer the questions with short answers. Beantworte die Fragen mit den passenden Kurzantworten.

1. Are you in Year 7, Holly? Yes, I am.
2. Are you nine, Holly? No, I'm not.
3. Is Jay a new student? Yes, he is.
4. Is Dave a teacher? No, he isn't.

Ziel 5: Ich kann eine Fotostory verstehen.

→ p. 31/5

Right or wrong? Tick ✓ the right box. Richtig oder falsch? Setze ein Häkchen ins richtige Kästchen.

	right	wrong
1. Luke can't find his bag.	☐	☑
2. Luke's phone is in the playground.	☐	☑
3. Olivia is in the park.	☑	☐
4. Luke's phone is in the park.	☑	☐

Ziel 6: Ich kann Informationen einer Schul-Website weitergeben.

→ p. 31/6

Lies die Informationen über die AGs an der TTS und beantworte die Fragen auf Deutsch.

Music Club for Year 7	Tuesday	Music room
Football for girls, Years 7 + 8	Wednesday	Playground
Music Club for Years 8–10	Monday	Music room
Art Club for Years 9 + 10	Thursday	Room 105

1. An welchen AGs können Holly und Olivia teilnehmen? an der Musik AG und Mädchenfußball
2. Welche AG findet donnerstags statt? die Kunst-AG
3. Wo spielen die Mädchen Fußball? auf dem Schulhof

Lösungen online
9a4d9y

Ziel 1: Ich kann über meine Schule sprechen.

Fülle die Lücken mit den richtigen Informationen über deine Schule aus.

I'm in Year (Year/~~student~~) 5. There's a playground (~~cat~~/ playground) at my school. We can play (play/~~open~~) games and talk there. There are classrooms (classrooms/~~flats~~) too. My favourite place is the cafeteria (~~caretaker~~/ cafeteria). We can eat (eat/~~close~~) there.

Ziel 2: Ich kann Aufforderungen im Klassenzimmer verstehen und äußern.

a) Welche Sätze drücken aus, dass du etwas tun sollst, und welche, dass du etwas nicht tun sollst? Zeichne entweder einen lachenden oder einen traurigen Smiley.

1. Open your exercise books, please. 
2. Don't talk, please. 
3. Don't sit next to Tim. 
4. Look at the picture. 
5. Don't play with your phone. 
6. Eat your food, please. 

b) Schreibe nun selbst zwei Sätze.

1. ☹ sing • in the classroom • please

Don't sing in the classroom, please.

2. ☺ look at • your book • please

Look at your book, please.

Merke:
Aufforderungen:
Look ....
Verbote:
Don't look ....

Ziel 3: Ich kann über meinen Schulalltag sprechen.

a) Finde die neun Wörter zu den Kategorien Personen in der Schule, Schulfächer und Tage im Buchstabensalat und umkreise sie.

G	T	H	U	R	S	D	A	Y	F	T	A
E	C	A	R	E	T	A	K	E	R	E	S
R	A	T	E	A	C	H	E	R	I	A	A
M	E	S	T	U	D	E	N	T	D	C	R
A	R	M	O	T	U	E	S	D	A	Y	T
N	T	H	B	I	O	L	O	G	Y	E	F

b) Schreibe sie in die richtige Spalte.

people	subject	day
teacher	German	Thursday
caretaker	Biology	Friday
student	Art	Tuesday

Fasse die Wörter in Gruppen zusammen. So kannst du sie gut ordnen und dir besser merken.

○ **Ziel 4: Ich kann auf Fragen kurz antworten.**

Verbinde die Fragen mit den richtigen Kurzantworten.

1. Are you in Year 7, Holly? → d. Yes, I am.
2. Are you eight, Holly? → b. No, I'm not.
3. Is Jay a new student? → a. Yes, he is.
4. Is Dave very good at spelling? → e. No, he isn't.
5. Is German your favourite subject, Jay? → c. No, it isn't.

a. Yes, he is.
b. No, I'm not.
c. No, it isn't.
d. Yes, I am.
e. No, he isn't.

Ziel 5: Ich kann eine Fotostory verstehen.

○ **a)** Wer kommt in der Fotostory in deinem Buch auf Seite 42 und 43 vor? Kreuze an.

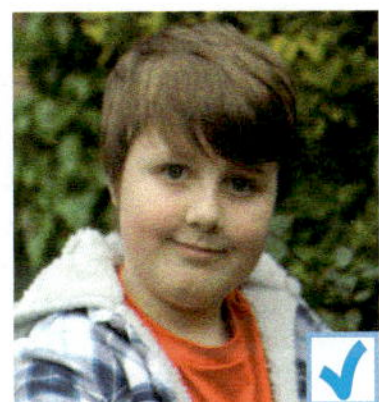

○ **b)** Ordne die Talente den Personen zu.

1. That's Olivia. 2. That's Luke. 3. That's Jay.

○ **c)** Wer gewinnt die Talentshow? Kreuze an.

Ziel 6: Ich kann Informationen einer Schul-Website weitergeben.

○ **a)** Welche Wörter geben dir Informationen über die Cafeteria? Kreise sie ein.

Art Club on Thursday	pizza on Wednesdays
Football for girls on Wednesday	lunch is in the cafeteria

Suche immer erst nach Stichwörtern, bevor du versuchst, die Fragen zu beantworten.

○ **b)** Beantworte jetzt die Fragen.

1. Wo gibt es Mittagessen? in der Cafeteria/Mensa
2. Wann gibt es Pizza? mittwochs

My free time

1
After school I listen to music.
2
Saturday
On Saturdays I help my dad.
3
At the weekend I go to the cinema.
Satur
Sunday
4
I have netball practice at lunchtime.
5
Sunday
On Sundays I play football.

48/1 **1 Put in the right words.**

music ✓ | cinema | practice | On Saturdays | football

7, 49/3 **2 (LISTENING) Right or wrong?**

a) Tick ✓ the right box.

	right	wrong
1. Netball is Luke's favourite sport.	☐	☑
2. At the weekend they have football games.	☑	☐
3. Luke's team is good at football.	☑	☐
4. After school Holly helps at an animal rescue shelter.	☑	☐
5. The dogs play with Sherlock.	☐	☑

b) Correct the two wrong sentences. (Lösungvorschlag)

1. Football is Luke's favourite sport.

5. The dogs play with Holly.

50/2 ## 1 Write the words.

1	2	3	4	5	6	7	8	9	10	11	12	13	14	15
BREAD	THINGS	WRITE	MATCH	SELL	DIFFERENT	STALL	EXPENSIVE	ALSO	MONEY	ORGANIZE	EVERY	CAKE	PRICE	TALK

A T T H E F L E A M A R K E T

1.

2. Rulers, pens and calculators are school ....
3. Holly: I ... the prices on the things.
4. There's a football ... on Saturday.
5. buy ↔ ...
6. The bags are ....

7.

8. £50 for a teddy? That's ...!

9. ... = too
10.
11. The TTS students ... a flea market.
12. There's a flea market at TTS ... year.
13.
14. How much is the ball? – Look at the ...
15. Please don't ...!

51/5 ## 2 Match the numbers and the words.

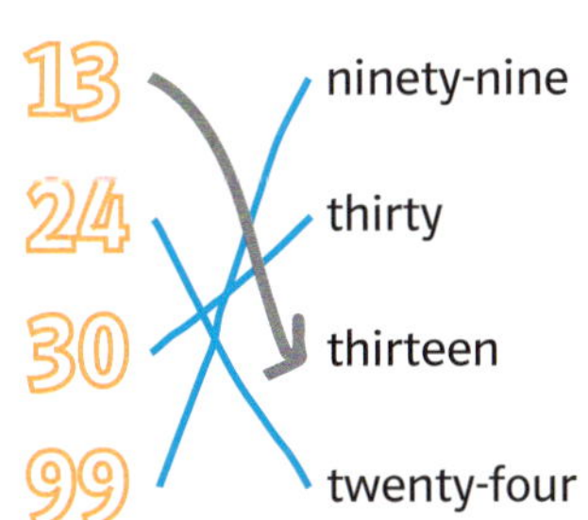

13 — thirteen
24 — twenty-four
30 — thirty
99 — ninety-nine

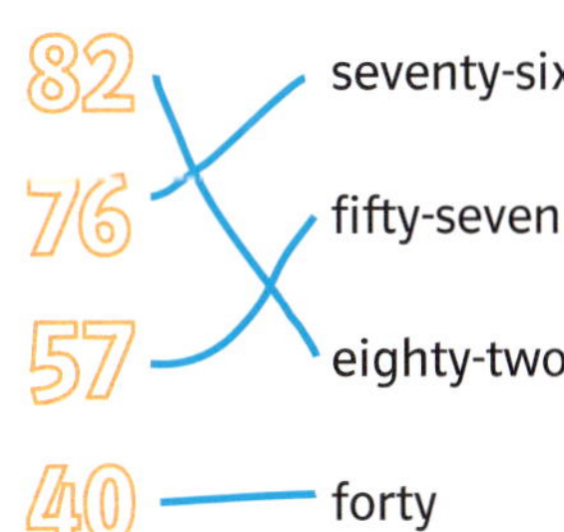

82 — eighty-two
76 — seventy-six
57 — fifty-seven
40 — forty

51/5 ## 3 (GAME) Play bingo in class. (Individuelle Lösung)

Schreibe sechs Zahlen von 1–100. Deine Lehrerin / Dein Lehrer liest Zahlen vor. Hake die ab, die du aufgeschrieben hast. Wer als Erste / Erster alle abgehakt hat, ruft „Bingo!“ und gewinnt.

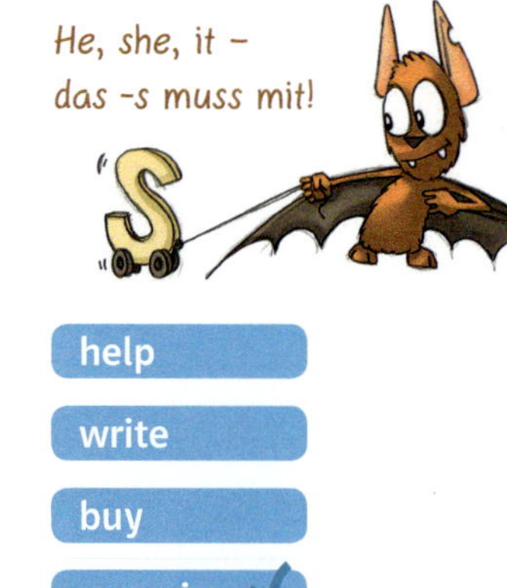

52/9 4 Complete the sentences.

help | write | buy | organize ✓ | sell | love

1. Every year Thomas Tallis School (it) organizes a flea market.
2. Dave (he) sells his DVDs.
3. Holly (she) writes the prices on the things.
4. Olivia (she) helps Holly.
5. Every year Mr Swindon (he) buys a lot of things at the stalls.
6. Mr Swindon (he) loves flea markets.

53/10a 5 Put in the right words.

1. Every year people go (go / ~~goes~~) to the flea market at Thomas Tallis School.
2. They buy (buy / ~~buys~~) a lot of things there.
3. Jay sells (~~sell~~ / sells) second-hand books.
4. And Olivia helps (~~help~~ / helps) Holly.
5. Olivia: I talk (talk / ~~talks~~) to the people.
6. Holly and Olivia: Yes, we like (like / ~~likes~~) the flea market. It's cool.

53/10b 6 Complete the sentences.

watch
go ✓
do
have
go
go
go
have

Achtung, bei diesen Verben musst du bei „he, she, it" ein „es" anhängen! Und aus „have" wird „has"!

1. Olivia's mum goes to the flea market every year.
2. This year Holly has a stall for cakes.
3. Dave has a stall for DVDs.
4. The money goes to Action World Hunger.
5. Luke and Jay sell school things. Then Luke does sport and Jay goes home.
6. Mrs Warren watches the flea market. She helps the students.
7. Then she goes to the cinema.

53/10 ## 7 Complete the sentences about Tim.

do | have ✓ | have | watch | love | play | like

1. On Mondays Tim has football practice. He loves football.
2. On Tuesdays he plays computer games with his friend David.
3. On Fridays he watches TV with his family. They like science fiction films.
4. At the weekend he does sport with his friends. They have a good time.

8 53/11 ## 8 (LISTENING) Listen to the dialogue and look at the picture.

8 a) Listen and complete the dialogue.

Kevin: I like the black and white football.
Tim: The football on the table or under the table?
Kevin: Under the table. Is the ball OK?
Tim: Yes, it is.
Kevin: How much is it?
Tim: It's £8.45.
Kevin: Oh, that's expensive.
Tim: But the money goes to a school in India.
Kevin: That's OK. I'll take it.

b) Draw more things in the picture. Then make a dialogue with your partner.

A: I like the blue bag.
B: Where is it?
A: On the table.
B: How much is it?
A: It's £10.
B: Oh, that's expensive.
A: Yes, but the money goes to Action World Hunger.
B: That's OK. I'll take it.

DVD | red box | black calculator | saxophone | ...
under | next to | behind | ...
£4.50 | £2.00 | £15 | ...
not expensive
the animal rescue shelter
a school in ... | ...

54/1

1 Write the words and crack the code. Who is it?

Thursday is my day. I go to my ★❇▲×›○▲ grandma 's house and she ○▲⊙☺✹ makes my favourite food – ⅄≈☼⅄⊙☺× chicken burgers and ⌘●✓○ plum cake. In the ☺❖☺×☼×★ evening I don't 💧▲×♦ want to go home. This is Michael.

I like Sundays. I don't ★☺♦ ✓⌘ get up at 7:30. My mother doesn't 💧†❇⊙ work. She has a lot of time. She ○▲⊙☺✹ makes a nice ⌖❇☺▲↗†▲✹♦ breakfast for us. At 11:30 I go to the animal rescue shelter. I ⅄†○☺ come home at 5 o'clock. At home I watch TV and then I go to ⌖☺› bed. This is Holly.

I don't have a favourite day. But on Sundays I go to a ⌖☼★ big shopping ⅄☺×♦❇☺ centre with my friends or we go to the ⌖☺▲⅄≈ beach. Then we do our ≈†○☺💧†❇⊙ homework. Sundays are cool! This is Pana.

a	b	c	d	e	f	g	h	i	j	k	l	m	n	o	p	q	r	s	t	u	v	w
▲	⌖	⅄	›	☺	↗	★	≈	☼	□	⊙	●	○	×	†	⌘	⇨	❇	✹	♦	✓	❖	💧

9
54/3

2 (LISTENING) Listen and tick ✓ the right answers.

1. 10:08 ☐ 8:10 ☑
2. 6:55 ☐ 6:35 ☑
3. 11:40 ☑ 11:14 ☐
4. 5:24 ☐ 4:25 ☑

10
54/4

3 (LISTENING) Listen and draw the times.

a) Listen and draw the times.

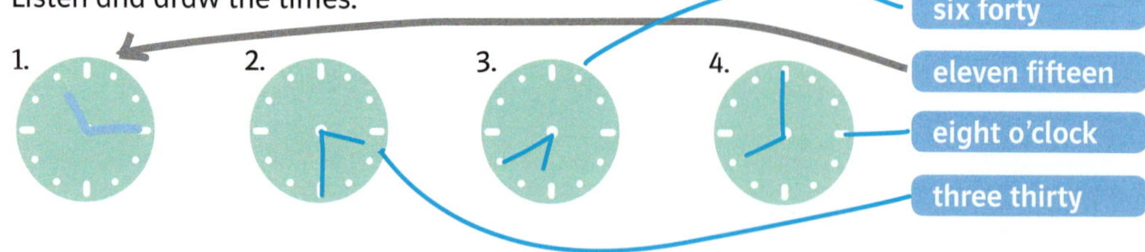

b) Draw four times for your partner. Then your partner says the times. (Individuelle Lösung)

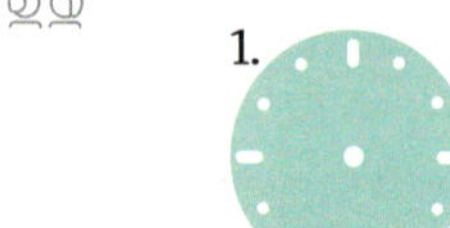
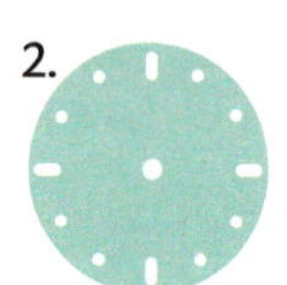
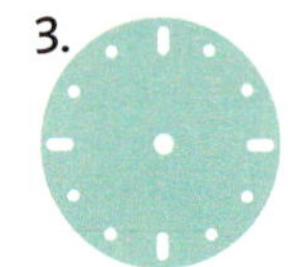
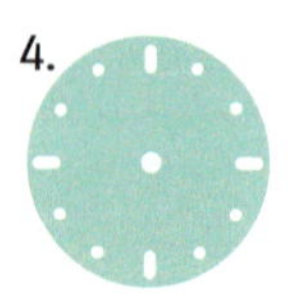

55/6 ↗

4 Make sentences about your day.

a) First match the verbs with the times. Add your own ideas. (Individuelle Lösung)

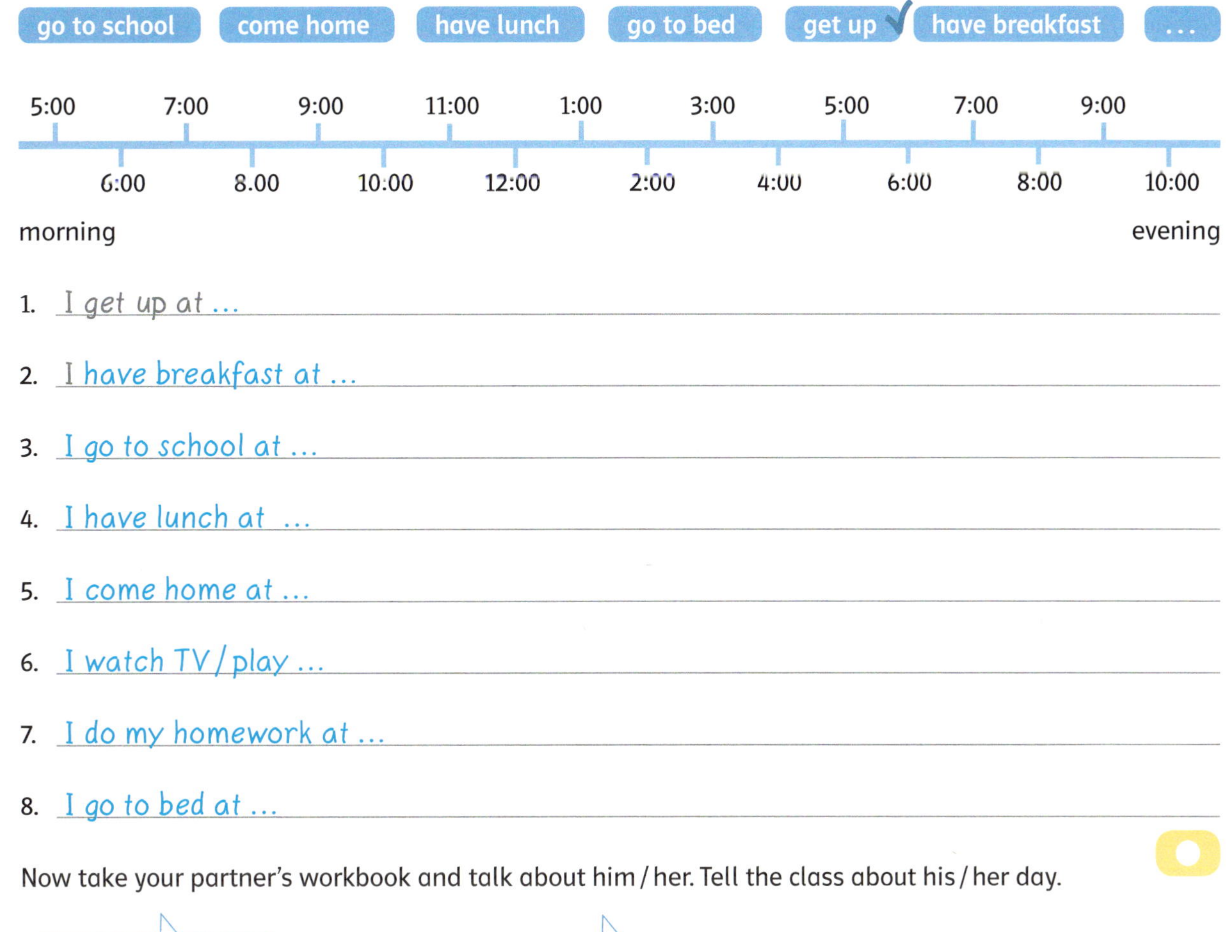

1. I get up at ...
2. I have breakfast at ...
3. I go to school at ...
4. I have lunch at ...
5. I come home at ...
6. I watch TV / play ...
7. I do my homework at ...
8. I go to bed at ...

b) Now take your partner's workbook and talk about him / her. Tell the class about his / her day.

56/9 ↗

5 Complete Holly's sentences. Use don't and the right verb.

don't + go, get up, do, go, make, have

On Sundays ...

1. I don't get up at 7:30 and I don't go to school.
2. I don't make breakfast. My mum makes it.
3. I don't do my homework on Sunday.
4. I don't have lunch at home. I buy a chicken burger.
5. I watch TV in the evening, but I don't go to bed at 8:30.

57/11a 6 Write about Pana. Use doesn't and the right verb.

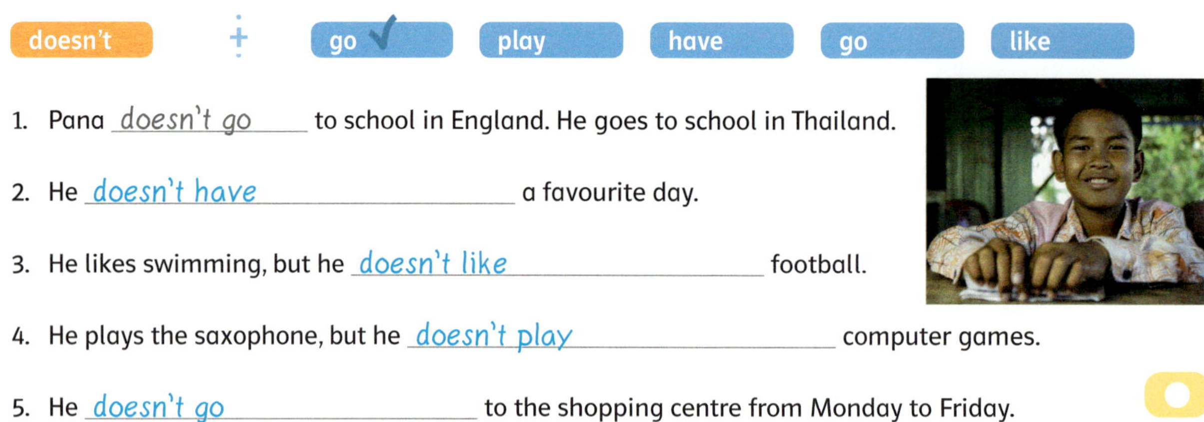

doesn't + go ✓ | play | have | go | like

1. Pana *doesn't go* to school in England. He goes to school in Thailand.
2. He *doesn't have* a favourite day.
3. He likes swimming, but he *doesn't like* football.
4. He plays the saxophone, but he *doesn't play* computer games.
5. He *doesn't go* to the shopping centre from Monday to Friday.

57/11b 7 What's right: don't or doesn't?

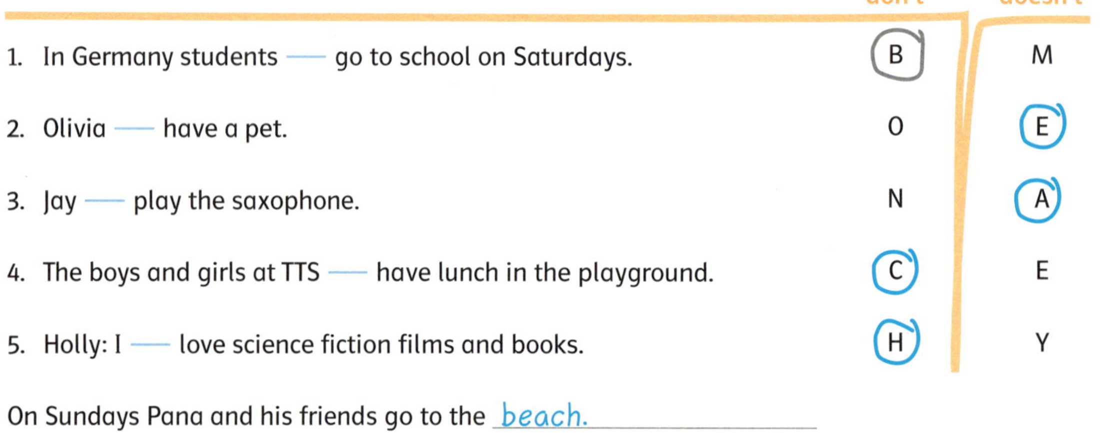

	don't	doesn't
1. In Germany students —— go to school on Saturdays.	(B)	M
2. Olivia —— have a pet.	O	(E)
3. Jay —— play the saxophone.	N	(A)
4. The boys and girls at TTS —— have lunch in the playground.	(C)	E
5. Holly: I —— love science fiction films and books.	(H)	Y

On Sundays Pana and his friends go to the *beach.*

❀ 8 (GAME) Who is it? *(Individuelle Lösung)*

57/12

a) Schreibe drei Dinge, die du magst, und drei Dinge, die du nicht magst, auf einen Zettel. Schreibe auch deinen Namen dazu.

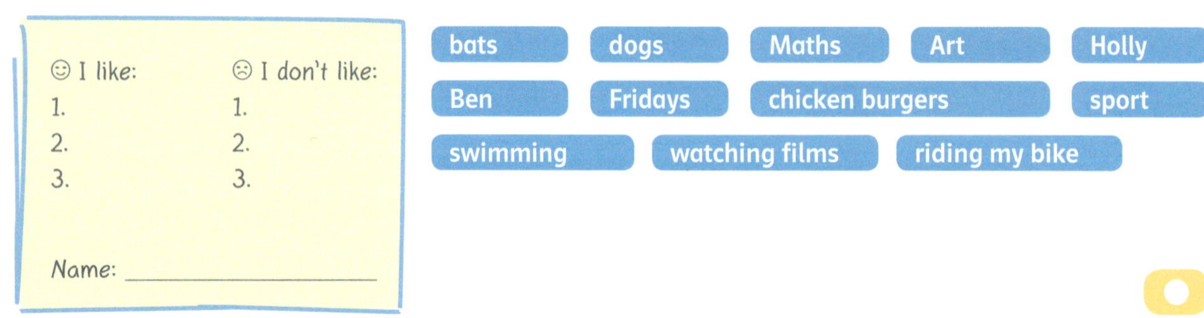

bats | dogs | Maths | Art | Holly | Ben | Fridays | chicken burgers | sport | swimming | watching films | riding my bike

b) Falte den Zettel und stecke ihn in einen Karton. Ein Schüler / Eine Schülerin trägt nun vor, was auf dem Zettel steht. Der Name wird nicht verraten. Die Klasse errät, wer es ist.

Lena: She likes riding her bike, English and dogs. She doesn't like Maths, science fiction films and Tuesdays. Who is it?
Jonas: That's Sarah.

58/2

1 Find the right words.

raccoon | police officer | attic | rubbish

1. police officer
2. attic
3. raccoon
4. rubbish

58/3

2 (READING) Put the sentences in the right order.

Luke and Sherlock find a hole in the rubbish bag. 3
Luke and Sherlock go to the snack bar. 1
Luke goes to the attic. 4
Mrs Abrihim talks to the police officer about the mess. 2
Luke can see a raccoon. 5

58/3

3 (READING) Right or wrong? Tick ✓ the right box.

	right	wrong
1. Luke and Sherlock play with Dave in the park.		✓
2. They see Mrs Abrihim and a woman at the snack bar.		✓
3. There's a mess in Mrs Abrihim's snack bar every day.	✓	
4. Sherlock finds a clue.	✓	
5. Luke can see a nice customer.		✓

60/2

4 (MEDIATION) Tick ✓ the right box.

Barbara Smith from Bristol in England has a great hobby. She collects comics. She has over 15,000 comics.

"I love my comics," Barbara says. "I read them all. My family does too. My favourite comics are about animals. I have 150 German comics too, and I love German animal comics."

1. Barbara Smith aus Bristol …
   a) sammelt Comics. ✓
   b) schreibt Comics. ☐
2. Insgesamt besitzt sie …
   a) 150 Comics. ☐
   b) 15.000 Comics. ✓
3. Ganz besonders mag sie …
   a) die Tier-Comics. ✓
   b) die Comics über Bristol. ☐
4. Ihre Sammlung umfasst …
   a) 150 Comics über Familien. ☐
   b) 150 deutsche Comics. ✓

Lösungen online
b5fb7b

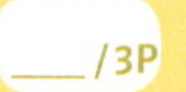
___/3P

Ziel 1: Ich kann über meine Freizeit sprechen.

→p. 42/1

Look at the pictures. What does Jayden do in his free time? Write four sentences.

help | listen to | play ✓  | watch

1. He plays football.
2. He helps his mum.
3. He listens to music.
4. He watches TV.

___/3P

Ziel 2: Ich kann mich nach Preisen erkundigen.

→p. 42/2

You are at a flea market. Complete the sentences.

You: I like the red pen. How much is it? – It's £7.50.

You: Oh, that's expensive. How much is a yellow pencil? – It's 45p.

You: That's OK. I'll take it.

___/3P

Ziel 3: Ich kann über meinen Alltag sprechen.

→p. 42/3

7:00 get up ✓ | 8:20 go to school | 8:30 go to bed | 4:45 play football

What does Jayden say about his day?

1. I get up at seven o'clock.
2. I go to school at 8:20.
3. I play football at 4:45.
4. I go to bed at 8:30.

___/4P

Ziel 4: Ich kann sagen, was ich (nicht) gerne mag.

→p. 42/4

Say what you and your friend like and what you don't like. (Lösungsvorschlag)

like / likes | love / loves | don't like / doesn't like

music | swimming | watching films | ...

I like / love music / football / ... but I don't like cats / Maths / ....

My friend likes / loves English / games / ...

but he / she doesn't like homework / ....

___ /5P Ziel 5: Ich kann eine Detektivgeschichte verstehen.

→ p. 43/5

A noise in the attic

It's 7:15 on Friday evening. Holly and her sister Amber are in the flat.

Amber: Can I have chicken burgers, please? I love burgers.
Holly: Yes, there are three chicken burgers on the table. One for you, one for Mum and one for me.
Amber: Great! Thanks!

A little later …
Amber: Oh, listen, what's that noise?
Holly: Where is it?
Amber: Is it in the attic?
Holly: Let's see.

Now it's 7:30 and Mrs Richardson is at home.
Mrs Richardson: Where's the noise?
Amber: In the attic?

Mrs Richardson and Holly are now next to the attic.

Mrs Richardson: I can't open it. It's locked.
Holly: But look, there's a hole!
Mrs Richardson: What can you see?
Holly: I can see Fluff and Honey in there!
Mrs Richardson: Fluff and Honey? In there? OK, let's go to the neighbours. They can open the attic.

Now it's 8 o'clock.
Holly: Guess what the noise is, Amber! Look! Fluff and Honey! But …
Hey! Where are the chicken burgers?
Mrs Richardson: Yes, Amber. Where are they?
Amber: I don't have a clue …
Holly: But I do, Amber!

Read the story. Tick ✓ the right box.

	right	wrong
1. Amber can have three chicken burgers.	☐	✓
2. There's a noise in the garden.	☐	✓
3. The neighbours can help.	✓	☐
4. Holly's pets are in a bag.	☐	✓
5. At 8 o'clock there are no chicken burgers on the table.	✓	☐

___ /5P Ziel 6: Ich kann Informationen über ein Hobby weitergeben.

→ p. 43/6

*Tushar Lakhanpaew from India collects pencils.
He has got more than 19,800 pencils in his collection.
They are from more than 40 countries all over the world.
"I like pencils," he says. "They are great. But I don't like pens."*

1. Wie heißt der Mann? Tushar Lakhanpaew
2. Wo kommt er her? aus Indien
3. Was ist sein Hobby? Er sammelt Bleistifte
4. Wie groß ist seine Sammlung? mehr als 19.800 Bleistifte
5. Was mag er nicht? Füller

Lösungen online
b5fb7b

Ziel 1: Ich kann über meine Freizeit sprechen.

○ a) Welche Wörter passen zusammen? Ziehe Verbindungslinien.

play | play with | listen to | help | watch | go to | help at

football | TV | music | my pets | the cinema | my family | an animal rescue shelter

○ b) Was machst du in deiner Freizeit? Schreibe nun zwei Aktivitäten auf. (Individuelle Lösung)

In my free time I ______ and I ______.

○ Ziel 2: Ich kann mich nach Preisen erkundigen.

Du führst ein Verkaufsgespräch. Hake die richtigen Sätze ab.

1. Du fragst, was ein roter Füller kostet.
   - a) How much is a red pen? ☑
   - b) Where is the red pen? ☐
2. Der Füller kostet £7.50.
   - a) At 7:50. ☐
   - b) It's £7.50. ☑
3. Du findest, dass der Füller teuer ist.
   - a) That's expensive. ☑
   - b) That's OK. ☐
4. Du möchtest den Füller kaufen.
   - a) I like it. ☐
   - b) I'll take it. ☑

○ Ziel 3: Ich kann über meinen Alltag sprechen.

Was machst du jeden Tag? Nenne auch die Zeiten. (Individuelle Lösung)

go to bed | get up ✓ | go to school | watch TV | have breakfast | play with my friends

1. Every day I get up at …
2. I have breakfast at …
3. Then I go to school at …
4. I play with my friends at … and I watch TV at …
5. I go to bed at …

○ Ziel 4: Ich kann sagen, was ich (nicht) gerne mag.

Trage die richtigen Wörter ein.

likes | love | don't like | likes

I love ☺ my pets. Fluff likes ☺ Honey and Honey likes ☺ Fluff but they don't like ☹ Sherlock.

Ziel 5: Ich kann eine Detektivgeschichte verstehen.

○ a) Lies noch einmal die Detektivgeschichte auf Seite 58/59 in deinem Buch. Beginne mit den Zeilen 1 bis 7 und schau dir das Bild genau an. Was ist richtig?

1. Wer ist Frau Abrihim?
   - a) Ein Gast im Café. ☐
   - b) Die Besitzerin des Cafés. ☑
2. Warum ist der Polizist bei ihr?
   - a) Er will die Frau verhaften. ☐
   - b) Er will der Frau helfen. ☑
3. Was ist mit Luke und Sherlock?
   - a) Sie sind gerade vorbeigekommen. ☑
   - b) Sie haben Ärger mit der Polizei. ☐

○ b) Lies nun weiter (Zeilen 6 bis 14). Beantworte die Fragen mit Ja oder Nein und gib die Zeile an, in der du die Antwort gefunden hast.

1. Ist die Unordnung schon mal passiert? Ja Zeile 6
2. Helfen Sherlock und Luke? Ja Zeile 13

○ c) Lies den Text nun zu Ende. Setze die richtigen Namen in die Lücken ein.

1. Sherlock finds the clue. 2. Luke looks in the attic.

Ziel 6: Ich kann Informationen über ein Hobby weitergeben.

○ a) Lies den Text und unterstreiche die wichtigen Informationen.

Tushar Lakhanpaew from India collects pencils. He has got more than 19,800 pencils in his collection. They are from more than 40 countries all over the world. "I like pencils," he says. "They are great. But I don't like pens."

○ b) Hake nun die richtigen Antworten ab.

1. Tushar Lakhanpaew kommt aus …
   - a) Indien. ☑
   - b) den USA. ☐
2. Seine Sammlung umfasst …
   - a) mehr als 40 Füller. ☐
   - b) mehr als 19.800 Bleistifte. ☑
3. Diese kommen aus …
   - a) Indien. ☐
   - b) mehr als 40 Ländern der ganzen Welt. ☑
4. Er mag …
   - a) Lineale, aber keine Bleistifte. ☐
   - b) Bleistifte, aber keine Füller. ☑

Let's have a party!

A

August
Notting
Hill
Carnival

Dance in the street.

B

October
Halloween

Wear a costume.

December
Christmas

Buy a tree.

C

66/1 **1 Write the name of the month and the special day.**

67/3 **2 Complete the months.**

January	March	July
June	February	May
April	November	December
August	September	October

67/4 **3 Read page 66 in your book. Right or wrong? Tick ✓ the right box.**

	right	wrong
1. The Notting Hill Carnival is in August.	✓	
2. People dance in the streets at a Christmas party.		✓
3. Muslims get new clothes at an Eid party.	✓	
4. People get big presents at Halloween.		✓
5. People eat together at Christmas.	✓	

68/3 ## 1 Find the words.

clothes | dancers | sweets ✓ | birthday | sandwich | pizza | costume | invitation

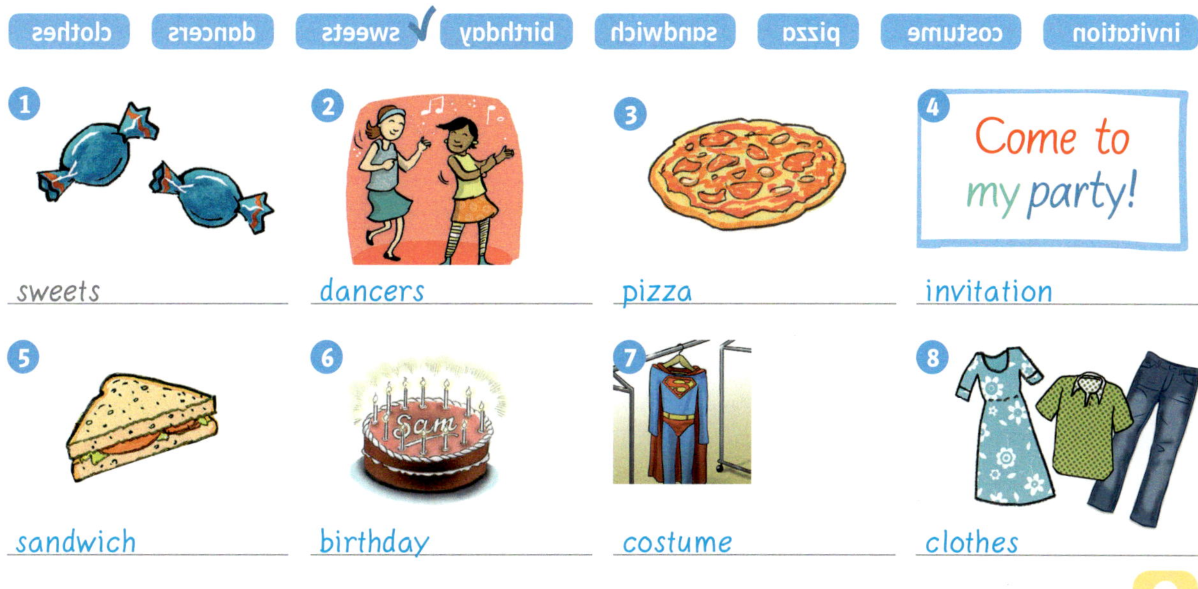

1. sweets
2. dancers
3. pizza
4. invitation
5. sandwich
6. birthday
7. costume
8. clothes

11 69/5 ## 2 (LISTENING) Olivia's message for Holly

a) Listen to the message on Holly's phone. Then complete the sentences.

1. Jay's birthday party is on Sunday.
2. Luke wants to buy a present and a costume.
3. Olivia and Luke want to go to the flea market.
4. They want to go on Friday at 3 o'clock.
5. After the flea market they want to go and have a pizza.

● b) Complete Olivia's question.

Do you want to come?

69/6 ## 3 Match the words.

a) Draw lines and make words.

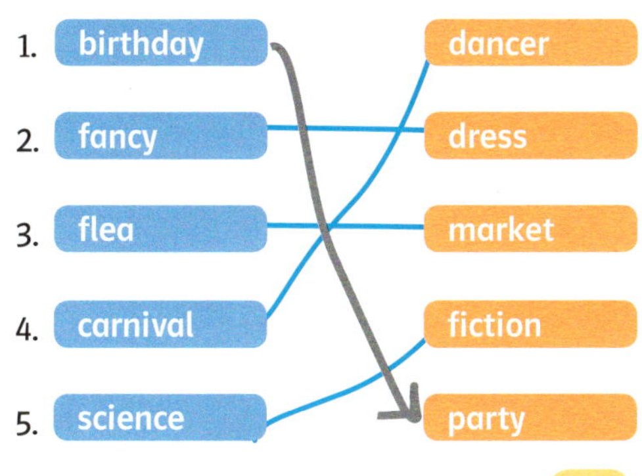

b) Write the words.

1. birthday party
2. fancy dress
3. flea market
4. carnival dancer
5. science fiction

70/8 ⊋
4 Ask your friend.

a) Write down the questions for a friend.

b) What does your friend say? Tick ✓ his / her answers.

Your friend's name: ____________

1. buy music from the internet • Do • you • ?
   Do you buy music from the internet? — ☐ Yes, I do. ☐ No, I don't.
2. you • Do • sing at home • ?
   Do you sing at home? — ☐ Yes, I do. ☐ No, I don't.
3. buy clothes at a flea market • you • Do • ?
   Do you buy clothes at a flea market? — ☐ Yes, I do. ☐ No, I don't.
4. you • Do • play football in the park • ?
   Do you play football in the park? — ☐ Yes, I do. ☐ No, I don't.

● c) Write three more questions for your friend and ask him / her.

70/9a ⊋
5 (SPEAKING) Talk about your teacher. (Individuelle Lösung)

Work in pairs. Write three questions about your teacher.

Partner A starts with the questions, partner B answers.
Partner B doesn't know the answers? Then ask your teacher.

Does he / she like music?
Yes, he / she does.
No, he / she doesn't.

Partner A: Does Mr Rader play football?
Partner B: Yes, he does.
Partner A: Does he like dogs?
Partner B: Hm. Mr Rader, do you like dogs?
Mr Rader: Yes, I do.
Partner B: Yes, he does.

read books on the computer?
watch TV in the evening?
play computer games?
have a brother or sister?
like dogs?
play football?
live in ...?

71/9b ⊋
6 Let's buy a present for Ben. (Lösungsvorschlag)

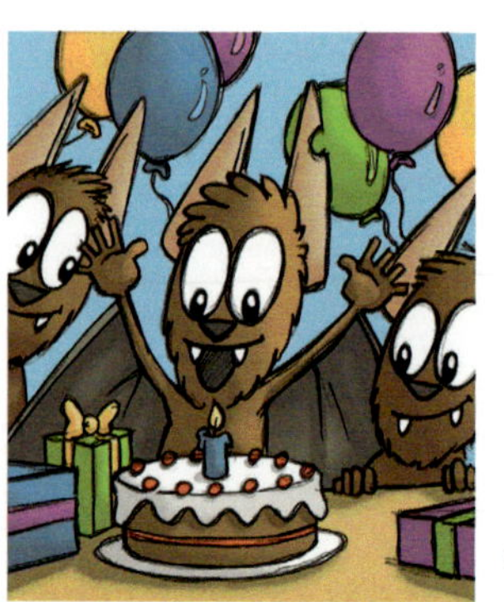

Ben likes costumes. Let's buy a cat costume.

Ben likes food. Let's buy chips / a pizza / a cake / ...

Ben likes sport. Let's buy a football / a netball / ...

Ben likes school things. Let's buy a pen / an exercise book / ...

71/10 7 **Make questions and answers about Ben and his friends.**

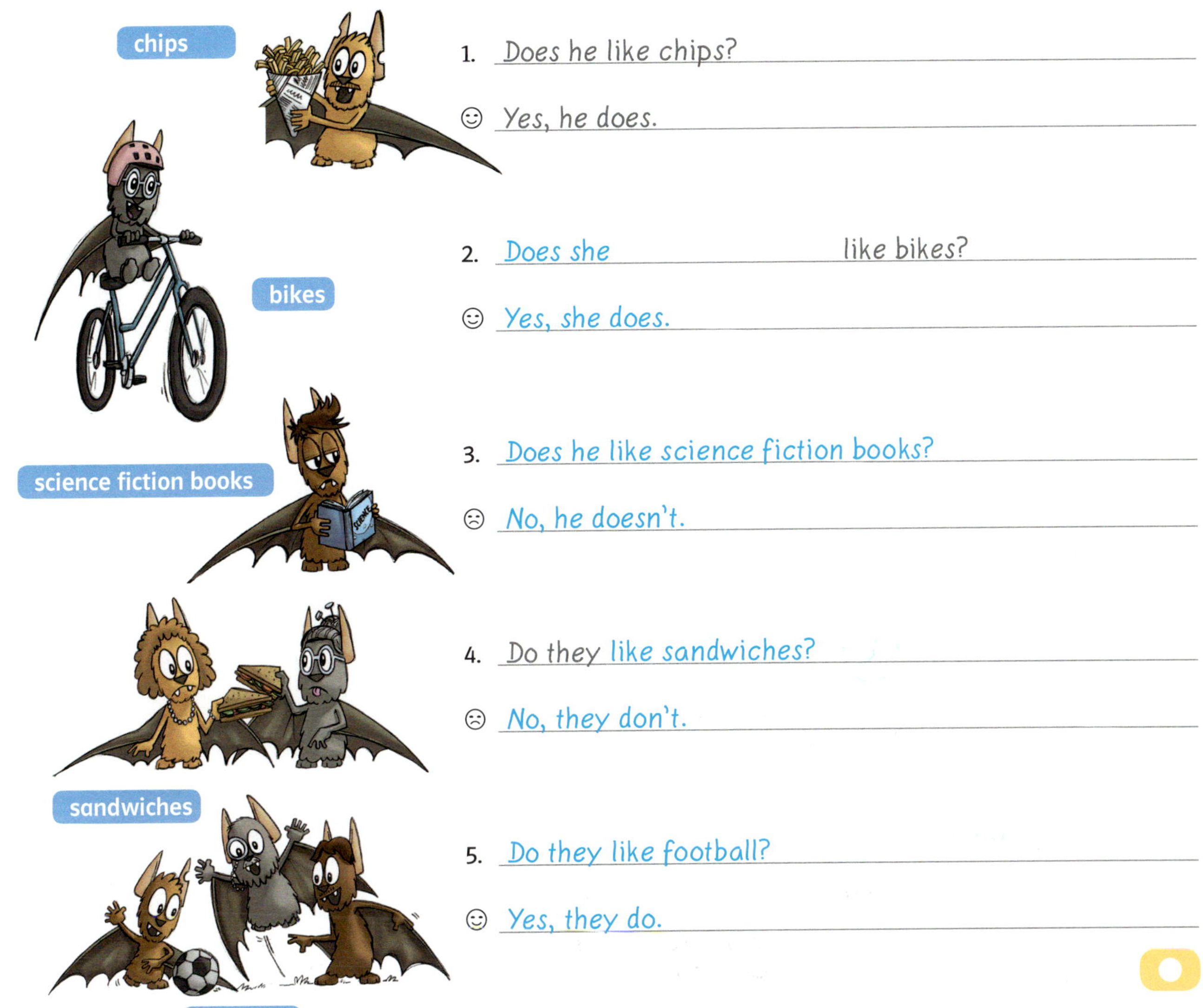

1. Does he like chips?
☺ Yes, he does.

2. Does she like bikes?
☺ Yes, she does.

3. Does he like science fiction books?
☹ No, he doesn't.

4. Do they like sandwiches?
☹ No, they don't.

5. Do they like football?
☺ Yes, they do.

71/11 8 **What about you? Put in the right question word. Circle your answers.**

what where when

(Individuelle Lösung)

1. What parties do you like? – School parties. / Parties with friends. / Family parties.
2. Where do you have your parties? – At home. / In the garden. / In the cafeteria.
3. When do you have parties? – On Mondays. / Every day. / At weekends.
4. What do you eat at parties? – Cake. / Pizza. / Chips.
5. What do you do at parties? – Eat a lot. / Play games. / Talk to my friends.
6. When do your parties start? – At 3 o'clock. / At 12 o'clock. / At 6 o'clock.

72/2 **1 Complete the mind map.**

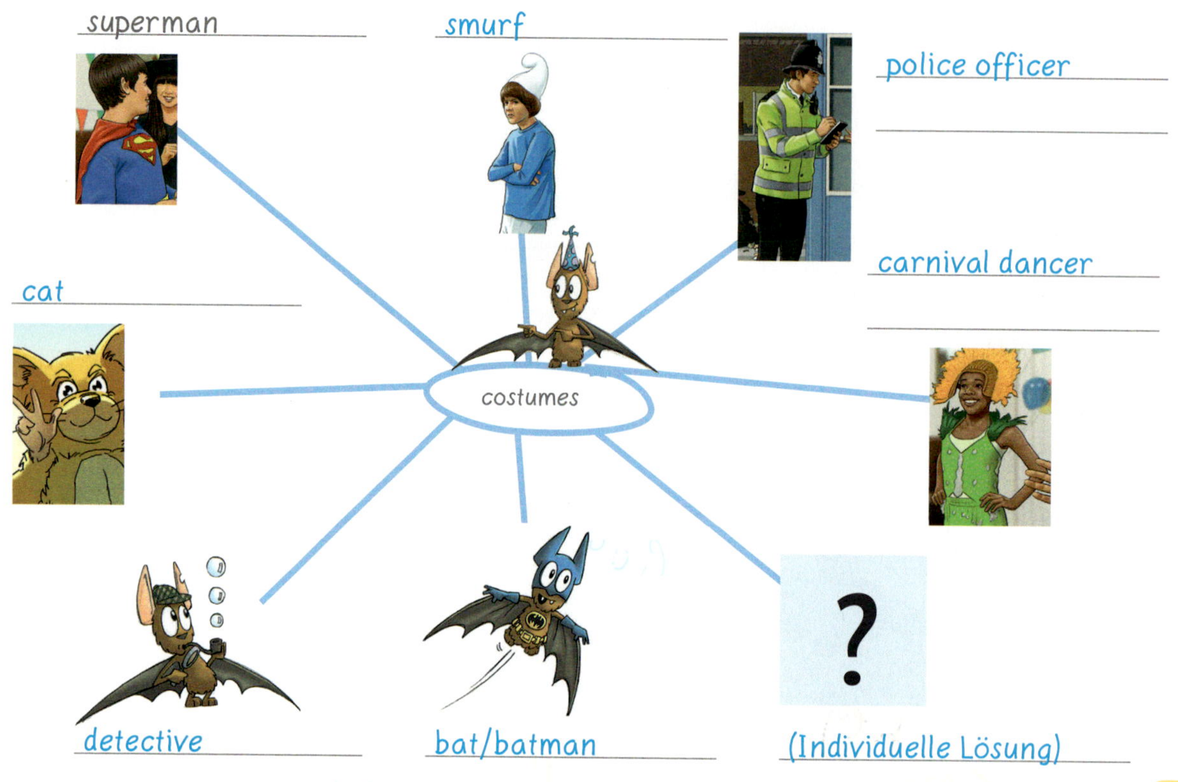

72/2 **2 Write the words.**

12 73/4 **3 (LISTENING) Listen and complete Olivia's shopping list.**

SHOPPING LIST

a bag of apples

10 tomatoes

6 eggs

cheese

orange juice

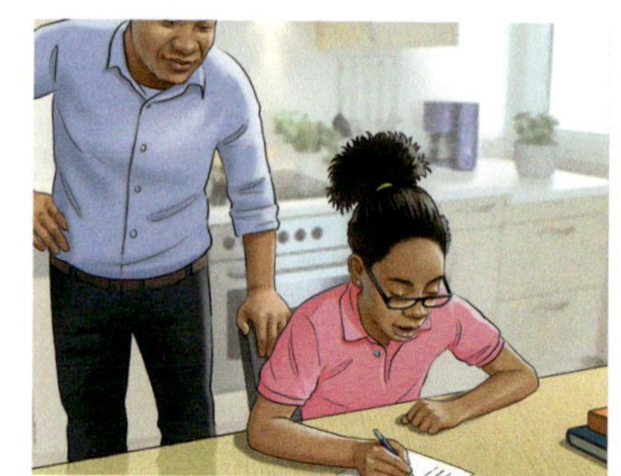

73/6 **4** How much food does Ben have? Look, count and write.

We can eat lots of fruit!
Achtung! Verwende „food“ und „fruit“ ohne „-s“.

5 boxes of apples

3 bags of oranges

2 kilos of bananas

2 boxes of eggs

3 bags of sweets

73/8 **5** Complete the dialogue. Then act it with a partner.

How much | Anything | That's | thank you | Here you | Bye | here you are | How can I help you | Can I have

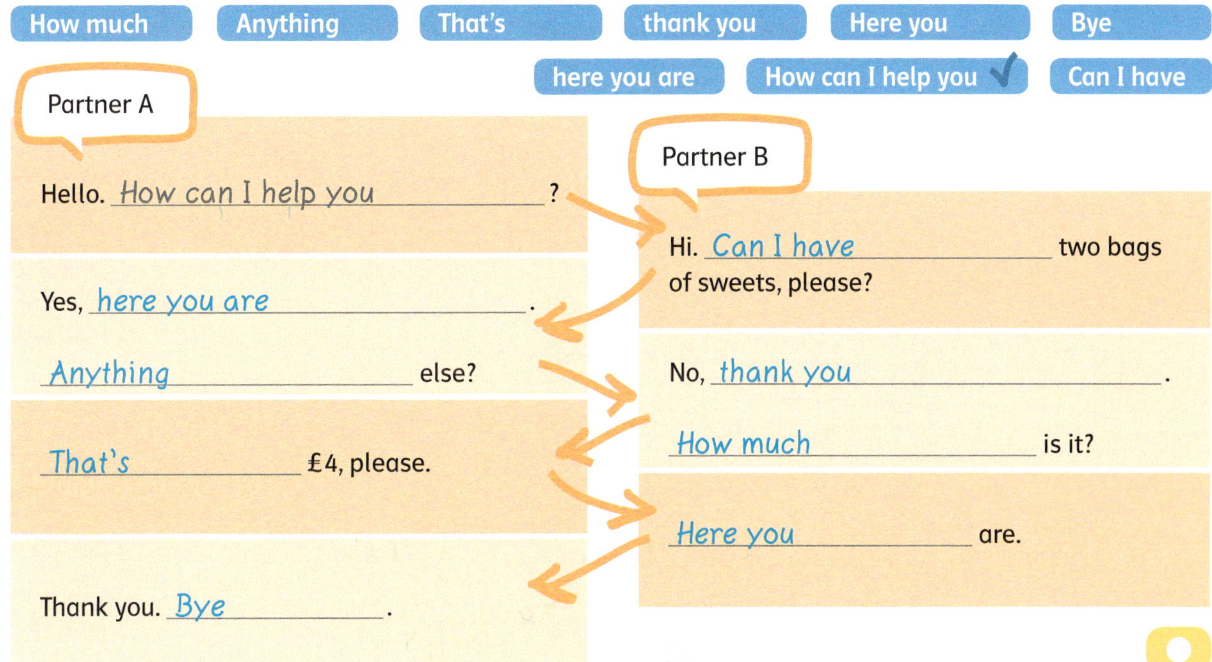

Partner A: Hello. How can I help you?

Partner B: Hi. Can I have two bags of sweets, please?

Partner A: Yes, here you are.

Anything else?

Partner B: No, thank you.

How much is it?

Partner A: That's £4, please.

Partner B: Here you are.

Partner A: Thank you. Bye.

74/10 **6** Choose the right words.

Mrs Elliot: Oh no, our (our / ~~his~~) house is a mess. But look! Here's Irina's phone.

Luke: No, it isn't. Her (~~their~~ / her) phone is red. This is my (my / ~~his~~) phone.

Mrs Elliot: And here's your (your / ~~their~~) football, Luke. Oh, isn't this Dad's book?

Luke: No, Mum, it isn't. His (~~her~~ / his) book is there on the table. Look! This is Irina's and my present for Dad's birthday. Our (~~his~~ / our) present for Dad is a new game.

Mrs Elliot: Great! Isn't Jay's party this Sunday? Do you have a present for Jay too?

Luke: No, I don't. Olivia and Dave have presents. Their (their / ~~his~~) presents are cool.

74/11 ↗ **7** Complete the sentences and questions.

my | your | his ✓ | her | our | their | his | my

1. Luke can't find his book. Luke: Where is my book?
2. Olivia and Holly can't find their pens. Olivia and Holly: Where are our pens?
3. Jay can't find his homework. Jay's teacher: Where's your homework, Jay?
4. Elena can't find her sandwich. Elena: Where's my sandwich?

● 74/11 ↗ **8** Put in the right words.

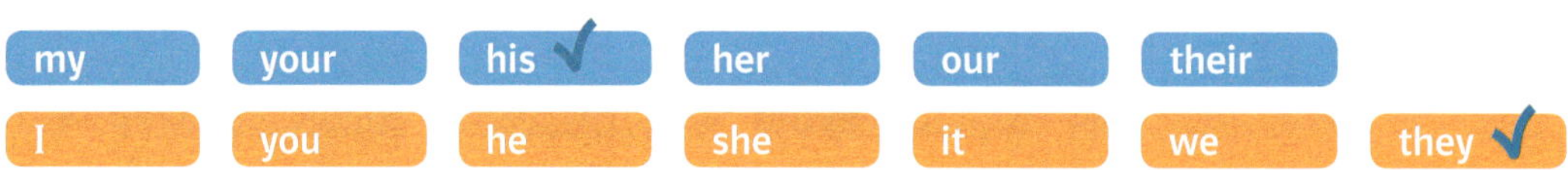

1. Leon the bat is Ben's friend. His birthday is on Sunday.
2. He has a lot of bat friends. They love fancy dress parties. Their costumes are great.
3. Lilly is one of Leon's bat friends too. Her present for Leon is a big birthday cake. She makes great cakes.

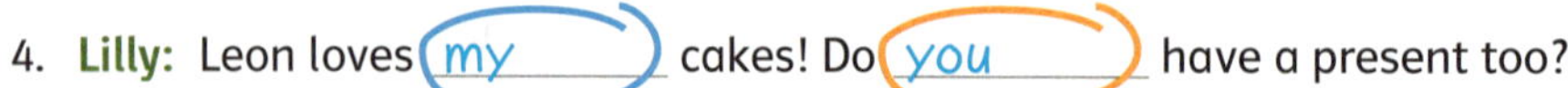

4. **Lilly:** Leon loves my cakes! Do you have a present too?
5. **Ben:** I have a bat game for Leon. He likes games.
6. **Lilly:** Oh, great. It's a cool game.
7. **Ben:** Lilly, we need music too. Can you play your saxophone?
8. **Lilly:** OK. I can play my saxophone and we can sing our favourite songs.

75/13 ↗ **9** Put the shopping dialogue in the right order.

Sieh im Buch auf S. 72 nach, wenn du Hilfe brauchst.

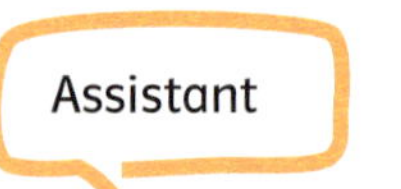

5 Yes, here are the oranges. Anything else?
7 That's £7.90, please.
3 Here you are. Anything else?
1 Hello. How can I help you?
9 Thank you. Bye.

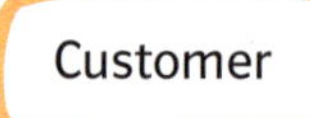

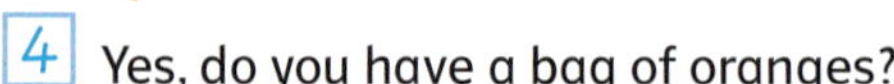

4 Yes, do you have a bag of oranges?
10 Bye.
2 Hi. Can I have two cheese sandwiches, please?
6 No thank you. How much is it?
8 Here you are.

76/1 1 Put in the right words.

assistant | closed | open | supermarket | change | hungry ✓

1. Are you hungry ? You can go and buy some sandwiches.
2. You can buy food and drinks at the supermarket .
3. You get your change from the assistant .
4. On Mondays the supermarkets are open .
5. But on Sunday evenings the supermarkets are closed .

77/2 2 Read pages 76 and 77 in your book and choose the right answers.

1. Jay and Shahid are at the supermarket …
   - a) because they need change. [ ]
   - b) because they buy drinks. [x]
2. The party is cool because …
   - a) the music is great. [x]
   - b) there are lots of chips. [ ]
3. Mr Moon rings the doorbell because …
   - a) he wants to dance. [ ]
   - b) the music is very loud. [x]
4. Later Jay's friends want …
   - a) a cheese sandwich and some chips. [x]
   - b) cakes and chocolate. [ ]
5. Jay and Shahid go to the new snack bar …
   - a) because the supermarket is closed. [x]
   - b) because they want to buy burgers. [ ]
6. Mr Moon's music is loud too because …
   - a) it's his birthday party. [ ]
   - b) his new snack bar is now open. [x]

78/1 3 (MEDIATION) Fasse die Informationen in Stichpunkten zusammen.

The Music and Art Festival

… takes place every year on the weekends in July. It's free. There are a lot of plays and films in the theatre tent. There's a big music stage in the park. People can listen to music and try food from different countries at the street stalls. Or you can go to the flea market and look at lots of interesting things. There's also a circus tent with a great circus show.

1. Wann findet das Festival statt?
   - a) jedes Jahr an den Wochenden im Juli [x]
   - b) jedes Wochenende im Jahr [ ]
2. Was kostet der Eintritt?
   - a) drei Pfund [ ]
   - b) der Eintritt ist frei [x]
3. Was kann man zum Beispiel dort machen?
   - a) Musicals anschauen, Musik machen [ ]
   - b) Zirkusshows anschauen, Musik hören [x]
4. Welche Veranstaltungsorte gibt es?
   - a) Theaterzelt, Musikbühne, Zirkuszelt [x]
   - b) Picknickwiese, Musikzelt, Zirkusbühne [ ]

Lösungen online
j8dj9k

____ /5P

Ziel 1: Ich kann über Feiertage und Feste sprechen.

→p.54/1

What can you say about these special days?

Halloween	in August	costumes
The Notting Hill Carnival	in December	presents
Christmas	in October	dance

1. Halloween is in October. People wear costumes.
2. The Notting Hill Carnival is in August. People dance a lot in the street.
3. Christmas is in December. People eat together and get presents.

Ziel 2: Ich kann mich über Partys unterhalten.

→p.54/2

Ask Tim questions about his birthday party.

1. get presents? ✓
2. play games?
3. wear costumes?
4. sing?
5. Where • you • live?
6. When • party • start?

1. Do you get presents? – Yes, I do. I get lots of presents.
2. Do you play games? – Yes, we do.
3. Do you wear costumes? – No, we don't.
4. Do you sing (at your parties)? – Sometimes we do.
5. Where do you live? – I live in 11 Henry Street.
6. When does your party start? – My party starts at five o'clock.

Ziel 3: Ich kann ein Einkaufsgespräch führen.

→p.54/3

You are in a supermarket. Complete the sentences.

1. **Assistant:** Hello. How can I help you?
2. **You:** Can I have two bags of sweets, please?
3. **Assistant:** Here you are. Anything else?
4. **You:** Yes. Do you have / Can I have a bag of apples?
5. **Assistant:** Yes, here you are. Anything else?
6. **You:** No, thank you. How much is it?
7. **Assistant:** That's £4.50, please.
8. **You:** Here you are.
9. **Assistant:** Here's your change. Thank you. Bye.
10. **You:** Thank you. Bye.

___ /6P

Ziel 4: Ich kann längere Dialoge verstehen.

→p. 55/4

In Mr Moon's snack bar

Jay and Olivia are hungry. They go to Mr Moon's snack bar.

Mr Moon: Hello Jay, hello Olivia. How can I help you?
Jay: Can I have a burger, chips and a cola, please?
Mr Moon: Yes. Here you are. That's £5.50, please.
Jay: Here you are.
Mr Moon: Thank you. And you, Olivia?
Olivia: Can I have an orange juice and a salad, please?
Mr Moon: Yes. That's £4.50.
Olivia: Thank you. But … Ah! There's a big snail in the salad!
Mr Moon: Hm. An orange juice and a salad with a big snail? Oh, that's £5.50.
Olivia: What?!
Jay: You're cool, Mr Moon!
Mr Moon: Sorry, Olivia. Here's a new salad for you.

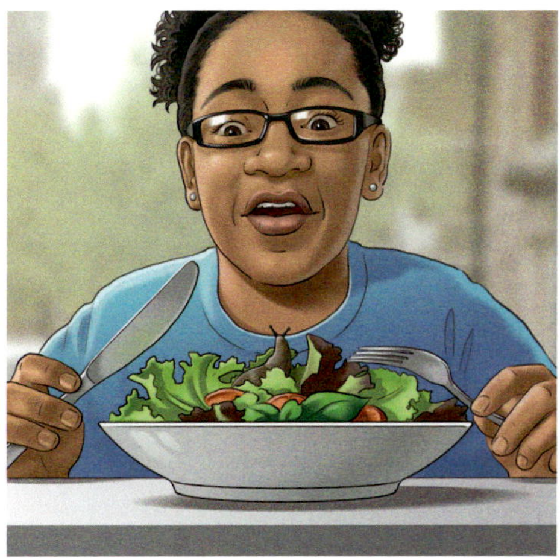

snail – *Schnecke*

a) Read the text. Then tick ✓ the right box.

	right	wrong
1. Jay buys a burger, chips and orange juice.	☐	✓
2. Olivia likes juice and salad.	✓	☐
3. Olivia finds an animal in her salad.	☐	✓
4. Mr Moon is cool.	✓	☐

b) Now read the text out loud to your partner. Try to show the feelings too. (Versuche beim Lesen auch die Gefühle darzustellen. Wann sind die Personen freundlich oder erschrocken? Wann sind sie leise oder laut, wann müssen sie vielleicht lachen?) (Individuelle Lösung)

___ /3P

Ziel 5: Ich kann Informationen über ein Stadtfest zusammenfassen.

→p. 55/5

INTERNET

The Bristol Festival takes place every year in June. There are plays, films and circus shows. There are two music stages. People can listen to rock music and to a classical orchestra. Lots of people go to the festival for a snack at one of the street stalls. You can buy sandwiches, burgers, salads and …

Lies die Fragen und unterstreiche die Informationen dazu im Text.

Beantworte die Fragen deiner kleinen Schwester zum Bristol Festival.

1. Wann findet das Festival statt? Jedes Jahr im Juni.
2. Was kann man dort tun? Theateraufführungen, Filme und Zirkusvorstellungen ansehen, Musik hören und z.B. Sandwiches, Burger und Salate essen

Lösungen online
j8dj9k

Ziel 1: Ich kann über Feiertage und Feste sprechen.

○ **a)** Schaue dir die Wörter an. Nimm zwei verschiedenfarbige Stifte und umkreise die Wörter, die entweder zu Halloween oder zu Eid passen.

a special day for Muslims | wear special costumes | "Trick or treat!" | October
people eat together | go to people's houses | boys and girls get new clothes and sweets

○ **b)** Lies die Sätze über Halloween und Eid und fülle die Lücken.

1. Halloween is in October. People wear special costumes.
   Boys and girls go to people's houses and say, "Trick or treat!".
2. Eid is a special day for Muslims. People eat together.
   Boys and girls get new clothes and sweets.

○ Ziel 2: Ich kann mich über Partys unterhalten.

Sarah feiert ihren Geburtstag. Vervollständige die Fragen an Sarah mit Do oder Does.

1. Do you listen to music? – Yes, we do.
2. Do you dance at your birthday parties?
   – Sometimes we do.
3. Does your mother make a cake?
   – No, she doesn't. We eat burgers and chips.
4. Where do you live?
   – I live in Schillerstraße 6, Nürnberg.
5. When does your party start?
   – My party starts at six o'clock in the evening.

○ Ziel 3: Ich kann ein Einkaufsgespräch führen.

Was antwortest du jeweils? Verbinde die passenden Fragen und Antworten.

1. Hello. How can I help you?
2. Anything else?
3. That's £5.99.
4. How much is it?
5. Here's your change.

a. Here you are.
b. That's £8.99.
c. No, thank you.
d. Can I have three bananas, please?
e. Thank you. Bye.

Ziel 4: Ich kann längere Dialoge verstehen.

Lies den Text. Achte beim Lesen auf die Gefühle der Personen. An welchen Stellen sind die Personen freundlich, erschrocken, besorgt oder entsetzt? Welche Gesichtsausdrücke passen dazu? Mach dir Notizen im Text und lies ihn dann laut einem Partner / einer Partnerin vor.

In Mr Moon's snack bar (Lösungsvorschlag)

Jay and Olivia are hungry. They go to Mr Moon's snack bar.

Mr Moon: Hello Jay, hello Olivia. How can I help you?
Jay: Can I have a burger, chips and a cola, please?
Mr Moon: Yes. Here you are. That's £5.50, please.
Jay: Here you are. (freundlich)
Mr Moon: Thank you. And you, Olivia? (interessiert)
Olivia: Can I have an orange juice and a salad, please?
Mr Moon: Yes. That's £4.50.
Olivia: Thank you. (freundlich) But … Oh no! Ah! (schreit entsetzt auf)
Jay: Olivia! What is it? (Jay ist besorgt und etwas ratlos)
Olivia: Mr Moon! There's a big snail in the salad! (ihre Stimme ist hoch)
Mr Moon: Hm. An orange juice and a salad with a big snail? Oh, that's £5.50. (belustigt)
Olivia: What?! (ihre Stimme kippt fast)
Jay: Ha ha! You're cool, Mr Moon! (Jay lacht)
Mr Moon: Sorry, Olivia. Here's a new salad for you.

Lies den Text laut. Wann liest du laut, wann leise? Musst du an einigen Stellen lachen oder schreien? Schreibe einfache Stichwörter an den Rand.

Ziel 5: Ich kann Informationen über ein Stadtfest zusammenfassen.

a) Finde die passenden Informationen und schreibe sie an die richtigen Stellen.

burgers | music stages | in the park | street stalls | salads | in August ✓ | sausages | circus shows | near the college | plays and films

GREENWICH SUMMER FESTIVAL

When: in August

Where: in the park, near the college

Activities: street stalls, music stages, circus shows, plays and films

Food: burgers, salads, sausages

b) Vervollständige nun die Informationen zum Greenwich Summer Festival auf Deutsch.

1. Das Festival findet im August statt.
2. Es findet im Park in der Nähe vom College statt.
3. Man kann Theaterstücke, Zirkusvorstellungen und Filme sehen. Und man kann essen und Musik hören.
4. Zu essen gibt es Burger, Salate und Würstchen.

People and places

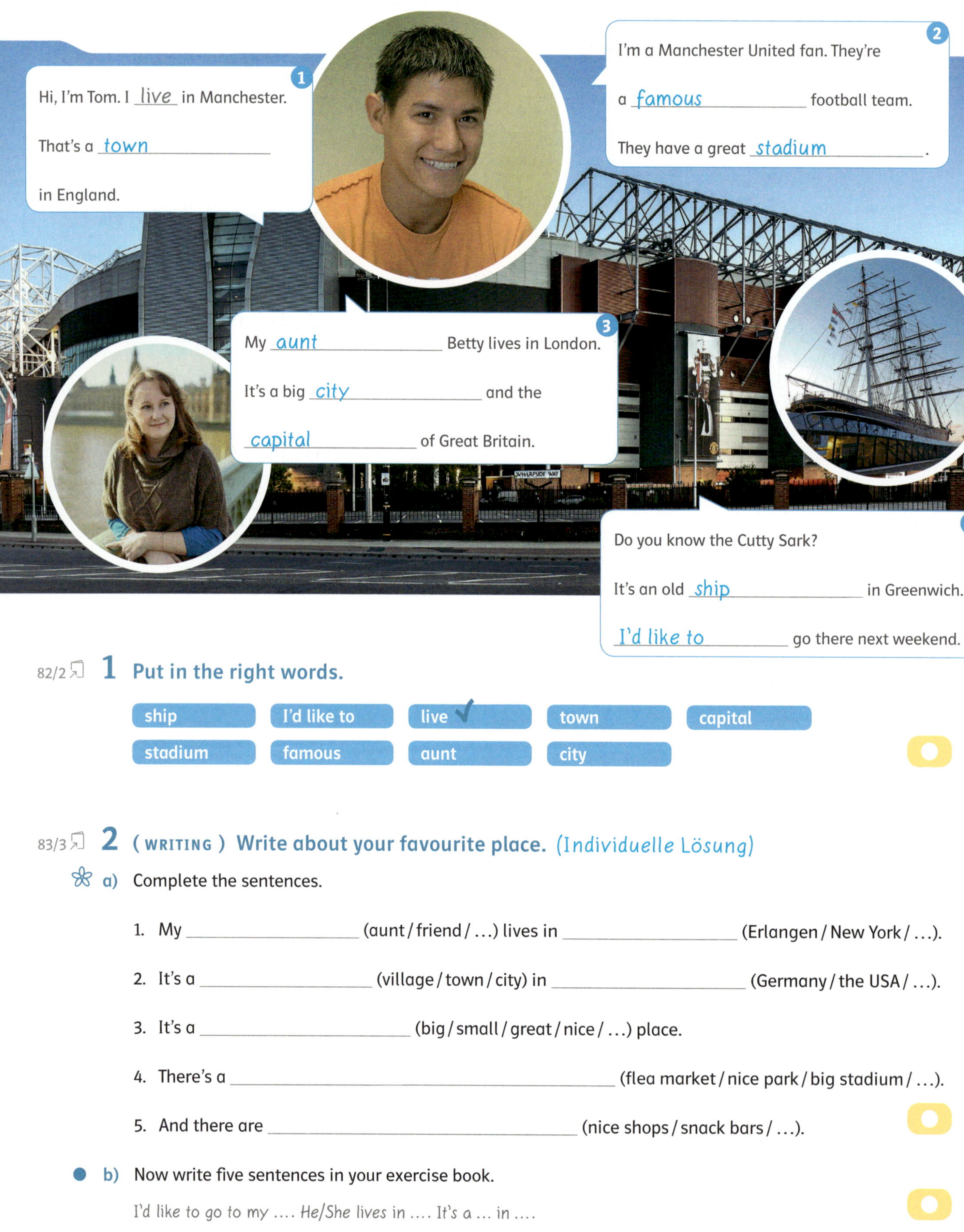

1
Hi, I'm Tom. I live in Manchester.
That's a town in England.
2
I'm a Manchester United fan. They're a famous football team.
They have a great stadium.
3
My aunt Betty lives in London.
It's a big city and the capital of Great Britain.
4
Do you know the Cutty Sark?
It's an old ship in Greenwich.
I'd like to go there next weekend.
WHARFSIDE WAY

82/2 **1 Put in the right words.**

ship · I'd like to · live ✓ · town · capital · stadium · famous · aunt · city

83/3 **2 (WRITING) Write about your favourite place.** (Individuelle Lösung)

a) Complete the sentences.

1. My ________ (aunt / friend / …) lives in ________ (Erlangen / New York / …).
2. It's a ________ (village / town / city) in ________ (Germany / the USA / …).
3. It's a ________ (big / small / great / nice / …) place.
4. There's a ________ (flea market / nice park / big stadium / …).
5. And there are ________ (nice shops / snack bars / …).

b) Now write five sentences in your exercise book.

I'd like to go to my …. He/She lives in …. It's a … in ….

84/1

1 Complete the crossword.

1	2	3	4	5	6	7	8	9	10	11	12
M											
O					B						
R		Y		S	L						
N		E		H	A		E	C	B	V	
I		S		I	C	T	X	E	R	I	F
N	D	T	L	R	K	I	C	N	E	S	I
G	R	E	A	T	B	R	I	T	A	I	N
	E	R	S		O	E	T	R	K	T	I
	S	D	T		A	D	I	E			S
	S	A			R		N				H
		Y			D		G				E
											D

1. evening ↔ …
2.
3. Today is Monday, … was Sunday.
4. not this weekend, … weekend
5.
6. The teacher writes on the … .
7. I want to go to bed. I'm very … .
8. Olivia's netball game was very … .
9. Let's go to the new sports … and play tennis.
10. Oh good. After this lesson it's … . Then we can go to the playground.
11. Let's go and … grandma this weekend.
12. I … my homework yesterday. So no homework today.

13
84/2

2 (LISTENING) Listen and write the right places.

at the sport centre | at the shopping centre | at a flea market ✓
at the cinema | at the swimming pool | in a classroom

1. at a flea market
2. at the swimming pool
3. at the shopping centre
4. in a classroom
5. at the sports centre
6. at the cinema

3 What can you do in these places? (Lösungsvorschlag)

85/4

I can play football.

1. At the sports centre I can play football / netball / …
2. At the shopping centre I can buy a lot of things / …
3. In the classroom I can write exercises / read texts / …
4. At the swimming pool I can go swimming / play with my friends / …
5. At the cinema I can watch films / meet friends / …
6. In the park I can play football / read a book / …

86/6

4 What's right: was or were?

	was	were
1. Sarah: Where — you last weekend, Tina?	M	C
2. Tina: I — at a talent show at our school.	O	I
3. Tina: The singers — good.	L	N
4. Tina: But my sister — great.	C	L
5. Sarah: — she the winner?	E	I
6. Tina: No. My brother — the winner.	R	O
7. Tina: His football tricks — special.	N	T

Where was Sarah last weekend? She was at a concert.

86/7

5 Match the sentences.

1. Dave likes science fiction films, but he
2. Luke and Jay like football, but they
3. The cakes at Holly's flea market stall
4. Olivia: I like the Notting Hill Carnival, but I
5. Holly likes shopping, but she
6. Luke: Our last Maths homework

a. weren't in the stadium last Sunday.
b. wasn't at the new shopping centre yesterday.
c. wasn't there last year.
d. wasn't easy, but Jay helped me.
e. wasn't at the cinema last weekend.
f. weren't expensive.

86/8

6 Use was / wasn't or were / weren't.

was / wasn't = Einzahl
were / weren't = Mehrzahl

1. Last Friday evening Holly wasn't at home.
   She was at the animal rescue centre.
2. On Saturday morning Luke and Jamie weren't at school.
   They were in Greenwich Park. They played football there.
3. Last Sunday Mrs Warren, the caretaker, wasn't at school.
   She was at home. She listened to her favourite music.
4. Lucy and Olivia were at the cinema last week. They liked the film very much.
   They weren't at the sports centre on Friday because they were tired.
5. Olivia wasn't at the Notting Hill Carnival last August.
   She was at the seaside with her family and had a great time.

14 87/10

7 (LISTENING) Listen to Sarah's Saturday.

a) Listen and put the pictures in the right order.

b) Now complete the sentences.

1. Last Saturday morning Sarah and Maya helped their mum with breakfast.
2. Then Sarah talked to her friend Tina. They organized a party.
3. In the afternoon Sarah and Maya worked a lot for the party.
4. The party started at 7:30.
5. Sarah and her friends listened to music and danced.
6. Then they watched a film on TV.

c) And you? Write three sentences about your last weekend. Draw pictures too. (Individuelle Lösung)

88/12

8 (SOUNDS) [aʊ] or [əʊ]?

15 a) Listen. Which sound is it? [aʊ] like in how or [əʊ] like in open? Tick ✓ the right box.

	[aʊ] how	[əʊ] open
1.	✓	
2.		✓
3.		✓
4.	✓	
5.		✓
6.		✓
7.	✓	

16 b) Listen, read and circle the [aʊ]-sounds and the [əʊ]-sounds in two different colours.

Sorry, but we don't know how to do our Maths homework today.

What about Rosie Brown?

She can show you how to do it.

89/2 **1** **Find the right words and complete the sentences.**

dad ✓ | salad | cold | beach | vegetarian | seaside | send

1. Last Sunday Holly and her _dad_ were in Margate.
2. They were at the _seaside_. They played frisbee on the _beach_.
3. Then they had some tea and a fruit _salad_ with lots of strawberries.
4. They didn't go swimming because the sea was very _cold_.
5. Holly didn't have fish because she is a _vegetarian_. She had chips.
6. They looked at some postcards in a shopping centre but they didn't _send_ any.

90/4 **2** **Complete the mind map.**

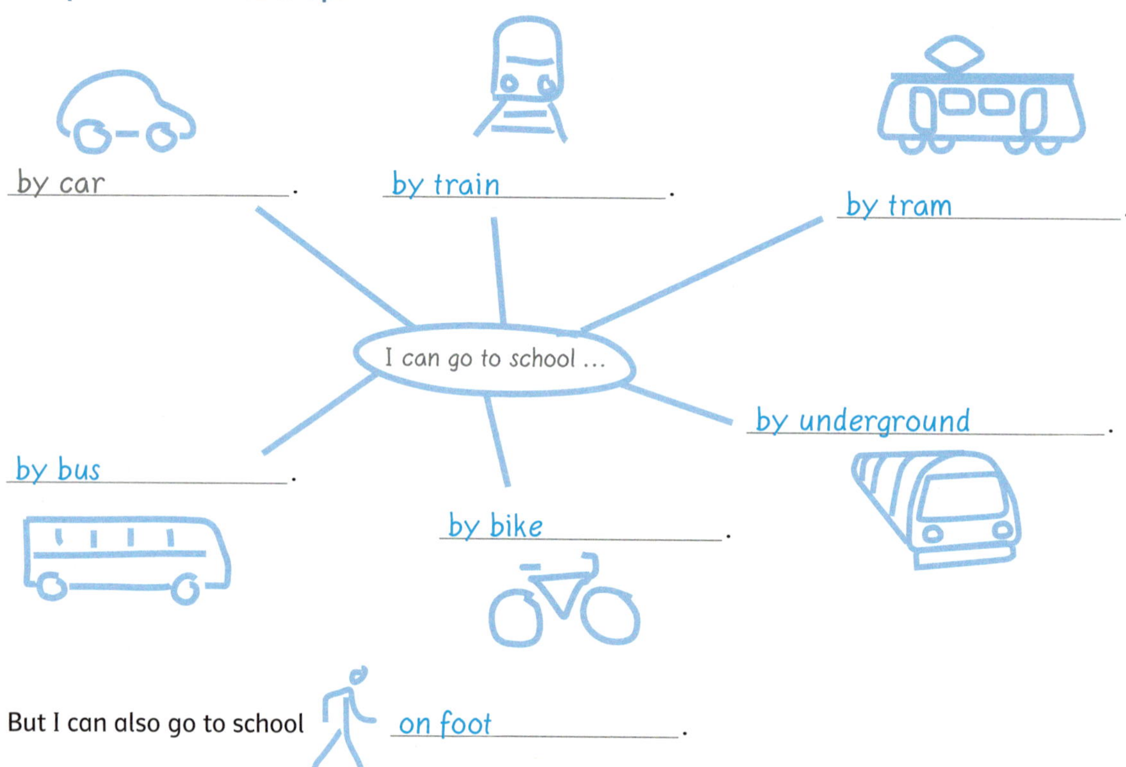

But I can also go to school _on foot_.

91/8 **3** (WRITING) **Write five sentences.** (Individuelle Lösung)

I'd like to go to … +
- Thomas Tallis School
- the new stadium in Greenwich
- Loch Ness in Scotland
- Vancouver in Canada
- India
- the USA
- …

\+
- and take a photo of …
- and talk to …
- and help …
- and take a snowboard to …
- and visit …
- and listen to …
- …

Example: I'd like to go to Thomas Tallis School and talk to Jay.

91/9 ↗ **4** Make sentences. Use went to and had.

	When?	Who?	Where?	What?
1.	Last weekend	Holly and Olivia	Margate	two fruit salads with bananas
2.	Last Saturday	the Fraser family	a snack bar	sandwiches
3.	Yesterday	Mrs Warren	the cinema	cola and some chips
4.	Last weekend	Luke and Dave	Jay's fancy dress party	great costumes

1. Last weekend Holly and Olivia went to Margate.
   They had two fruit salads with bananas.
2. Last Saturday the Fraser family went to a snack bar.
   They had sandwiches.
3. Yesterday Mrs Warren went to the cinema.
   She had cola and some chips.
4. Last weekend Luke and Dave went to Jay's fancy dress party.
   They had great costumes.

92/11 ↗ **5** Holly's weekend

did • go to Margate

did • go swimming • in the sea

did • play frisbee • on the beach

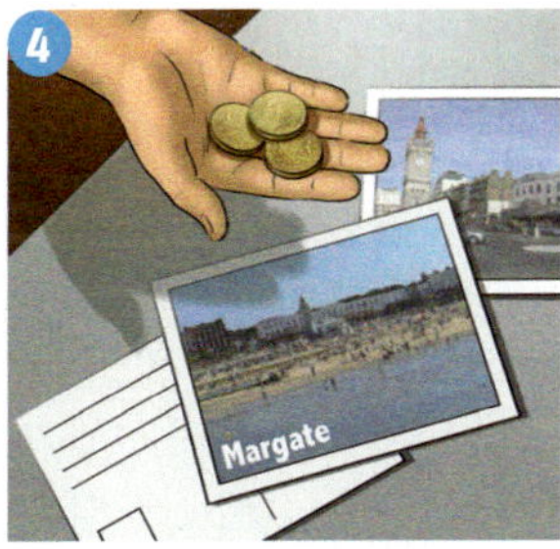

did • buy postcards

a) Look at the pictures and write questions with did. The words under the pictures can help you.

b) Read page 89 in your book again and answer the questions with Yes, she did. or No, she didn't.

1. Did Holly go to Margate? – Yes, she did.
2. Did she go swimming in the sea? – No, she didn't.
3. Did she play frisbee on the beach? – Yes, she did.
4. Did she buy postcards? – No, she didn't.

92/14 ## 6 Put in the right question words.

Dave asks Jay about his weekend. Put What, Where, Why or How in Dave's questions.

1. Where did you go on Saturday? – I went to the park.
2. How did you go to the park? – I went there by bike.
3. What did you play in the park? – I played football with my friends.
4. Where did you go then? – I went home.
5. Why did you go home? – I went home because I was hungry.

93/15 ## 7 Complete Olivia's questions. Luke's answers can help you.

1. Where did you go at the weekend, Luke? – I went to Greenwich Park.
2. What did you play in the park? – I played frisbee with Sherlock.
3. Where did you go after? – We went to a snack bar.
4. What did you have there? – I had a big sandwich.
5. And what did Sherlock have? – Sherlock had some dog food. He liked it.

8 (SPEAKING) Complete the dialogue. Then act it with a partner. (Lösungsvorschlag)

93/16

Partner A

Where did you go last weekend?
(Wo bist du letztes Wochenende hingefahren?)

Partner B

We went to ______
(Wir waren in ….)

Partner A

When did you go?
(Wann seid ihr dort hingefahren?)

Partner B

We went on Saturday / Sunday
(Wir sind am Samstag/Sonntag gefahren.)

Partner A

How did you go there?
(Wie seid ihr hingefahren?)

Partner B

We went by car / train / ….
(Wir sind mit … gefahren.)

Partner A

What did you do there?
(Was habt ihr dort gemacht?)

Partner B

We visited my aunt / ….
We played frisbee / … in a park.
(Wir haben … besucht. / Wir haben ….)

Partner A

Did you like it?
(Hat es dir gefallen?)

Partner B

Yes, it was …. / No, it wasn't great / ….
(Ja, es war …. / Nein, es war nicht ….)

94/2 ## 1 (GAME) Word bingo (Individuelle Lösung)

Bildet zu viert oder fünft Gruppen. Einer/Eine ist „the caller“ (der/die Ansager/in). Die anderen kreisen jeweils auf ihren Karten verdeckt fünf Vokabeln ein. Jetzt nennt „the caller“ einige der Vokabeln auf Deutsch. Haben die anderen das entsprechende englische Wort eingekreist, haken sie es ab. Wer zuerst fünf Häkchen hat, ruft „Bingo!“ und gewinnt.

hate	be sick	diary	first mate
man overboard	water	put	stay
happy	hot	awful	scared
shark	shout	arrive	man
job	storm	one day	great-great-grandad

95/4 ## 2 Read pages 94 and 95 in your book and put the sentences in the right order.

6	They arrived in Australia in June.	A	7	There were some big sharks in the sea.	R
5	Rodney was OK, but he was scared.	C	8	Jim put bags of wool on the Cutty Sark.	D
2	Jim was sick in the first weeks.	O	4	Rodney, the first mate, went overboard.	T
1	Jim started his job on the Cutty Sark in April 1885.	P	3	There were a lot of storms on the trip to Australia.	S

Now put the letters in the right order to find a word: postcard

96/3 ## 3 (MEDIATION) Greenwich Park (Lösungsvorschlag)

Deine Oma hat den Text im Internet gefunden, aber sie versteht ihn nicht. Kannst du ihr helfen?

INTERNET

Greenwich Park

Greenwich Park is one of London's beautiful eight parks. There are a lot of very nice gardens. Come and sit under an old tree, have a picnic, chill out or play frisbee. Why not go to the Meridian Line? It's interesting! Greenwich Park is open every day – from 6 o'clock in the morning.

1. Was steht da über Picknick? Darf man das? ja, das wird sogar vorgeschlagen
2. Was kann man noch im Park tun? sich unter einen der alten Bäume setzen, ausruhen, Frisbee spielen
3. Wird etwas besonders empfohlen? ja, die Meridian Line (der Nullmeridian)
4. Wann genau ist der Park geöffnet? täglich ab 6 Uhr morgens

Lösungen online 48sd4t

___/4P Ziel 1: Ich kann einen Ort vorstellen. (Individuelle Lösung)

→p. 66/1

Complete the sentences. The words can help you.

My name is ______________________.

I live in (1) ______________________.

It's (2) ____________ (3) ____________.

There's a (4) ______________________

and there are a lot of (4) ______________________.

(1) Regensburg · Bayreuth · Lindau · Bavaria · ...

(2) a small · a big · a great · an interesting · an old · ...

(3) town · city · village

(4) school(s) · cinema(s) · park(s) · sports centre(s) · shop(s) · ...

___/4P Ziel 2: Ich kann über das vergangene Wochenende sprechen.

→p. 66/2

What did Jay say about his weekend? Finish the sentences. Use the simple past.

go to Dave's house · have breakfast with my family · do my homework · play football

1. On Saturday morning I had breakfast with my family.
2. Then I went to Dave's house.
3. We played football.
4. In the afternoon I did my homework.

___/4P Ziel 3: Ich kann mich über einen Tagesausflug unterhalten.

→p. 66/3

Write what Charlotte says about her trip to Margate with her mum and dad.

go to Margate • train

look at postcards • shop

go swimming • sea

have • fish and chips

1. We went to Margate by train.
2. I looked at postcards in a shop.
3. I went swimming in the sea.
4. We had (some) fish and chips.

Ziel 4: Ich kann Auszüge aus einem Tagebuch verstehen.

→p.67/4

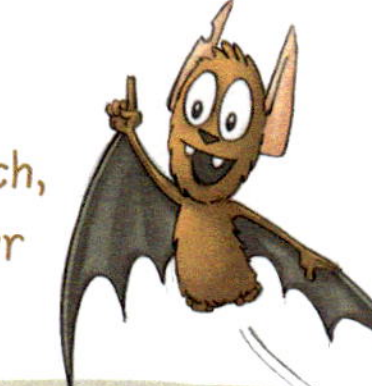

Lies den Text mehrfach, dann ist Vieles leichter zu verstehen.

Read the pages from Jessie's diary and answer the questions.

Saturday, 4th May

Yesterday I went to London by train. My sister Gemma lives there. First we went to a big book shop. I looked at some books about London, but I didn't buy one. They were very expensive. After that we went to the Cutty Sark in Greenwich by bus. It's a very old and interesting ship. In the evening we had fish and chips in a nice snack bar. What a cool day!

Sunday, 5th May

My last day in London. Gemma and I had breakfast at nine o'clock. Then we went to the city centre by underground. We went to a cinema in Oxford Street. Daniel Radcliffe was there, the famous Harry Potter. We wanted to talk to Daniel, but there were lots of people around him. Now I'm home again with my mum, my dad and my dog Daniel. I'm happy I can talk to this Daniel.

(Lösungsvorschlag)

1. What day did Jessie go to London? On Friday.
2. Did Jessie buy a book? Why/Why not? No, she didn't because they were very expensive.
3. What did they have in the evening? They had fish and chips.
4. How did they go to the city centre? They went by underground.
5. Did the girls talk to Daniel Radcliffe? No, they didn't. (There were a lot of people.)
6. Why is Jessie happy now? Because she can talk to her dog Daniel.

Ziel 5: Ich kann touristische Informationen über Greenwich weitergeben.

→p.67/5

Hilf einer Touristin, die am Schalter mit einem Mann der Touristeninformation sprechen möchte.

(Lösungsvorschlag)

Frau: Kannst du bitte fragen, wann ich auf die Cutty Sark gehen kann?

Du: When can she go on the Cutty Sark?

Mann: Every day from ten to five o'clock.

Du: Jeden Tag zwischen zehn Uhr (morgens) und fünf Uhr (am Nachmittag).

Frau: Wie kann ich nach Greenwich fahren?

Du: How can she go to Greenwich?

Mann: There's the train, the underground and there are a lot of buses too.

Du: Man kann mit der Bahn oder der U-Bahn fahren. Es gibt außerdem viele Busse.

Lösungen online 48sd4t

Ziel 1: Ich kann einen Ort vorstellen.

○ **a)** Welche Wörter brauchst du, um über deinen Wohnort zu sprechen? Kreise sie farbig ein.

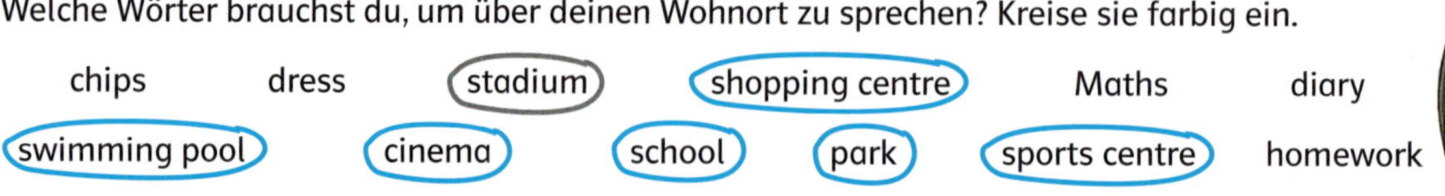

chips
dress
stadium
shopping centre
Maths
diary
swimming pool
cinema
school
park
sports centre
homework

○ **b)** Schreibe drei Sätze über eine Stadt (es kann dein Wohnort sein). Du kannst die umkreisten Wörter in a) und die Wörter unten benutzen. (Individuelle Lösung)

There's / There are …
My favourite place is …
… next to …
… in …
1. My favourite place is
2. There's
3.

Ziel 2: Ich kann über das vergangene Wochenende sprechen.

○ **a)** Verbinde die Verben mit ihren Formen im simple past.

○ **b)** Vervollständige nun den Text.

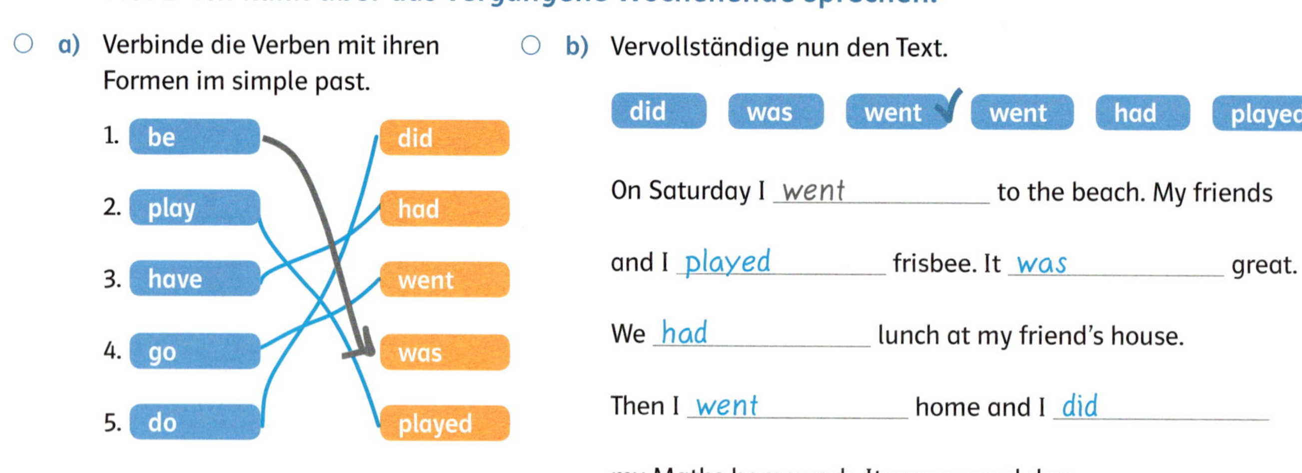

and I played frisbee. It was great.
We had lunch at my friend's house.
Then I went home and I did
my Maths homework. It was a good day.

○ Ziel 3: Ich kann mich über einen Tagesausflug unterhalten.

Trage diese Wörter in die richtige Zeile ein.

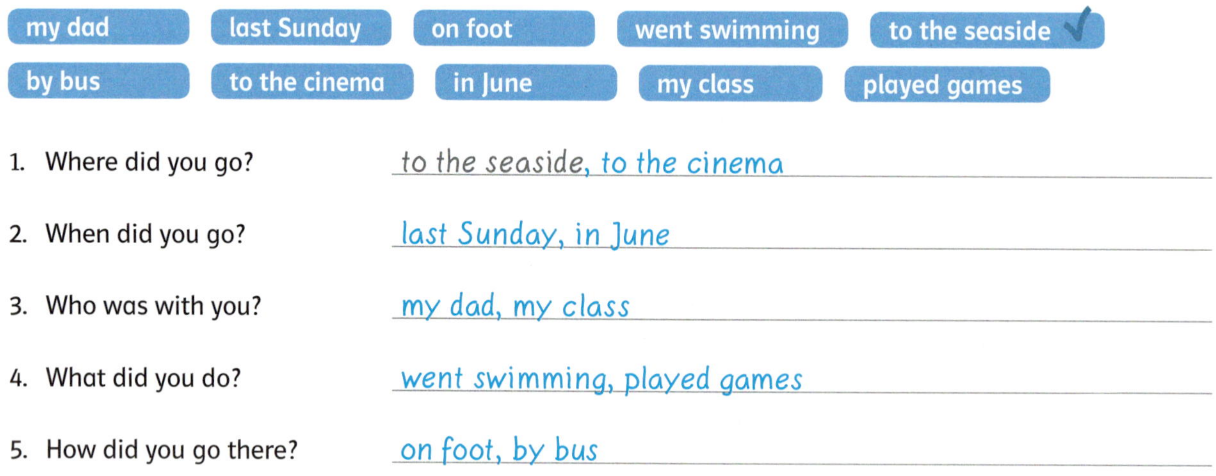

my dad
last Sunday
on foot
went swimming
to the seaside
by bus
to the cinema
in June
my class
played games
1. Where did you go? to the seaside, to the cinema
2. When did you go? last Sunday, in June
3. Who was with you? my dad, my class
4. What did you do? went swimming, played games
5. How did you go there? on foot, by bus

Ziel 4: Ich kann Auszüge aus einem Tagebuch verstehen.

Saturday, 4th May

Yesterday I went to London by train. My sister Gemma lives there. We went to a big book shop. I looked at books about London, but I didn't buy one. They were very expensive. Then we went to the Cutty Sark in Greenwich. It's a very old and interesting ship. In the evening we had fish and chips in a nice snack bar. What a cool day!

Sunday, 5th May

My last day in London. Gemma and I had breakfast at nine o'clock. Then we went to the city centre by underground. We went to a cinema. Daniel Radcliffe was there, the famous Harry Potter. We wanted to talk to Daniel, but there were a lot of people around him.

○ **a)** Was haben Jessie und ihre Schwester in London unternommen? Setze vier Haken.

Sie waren im Buchladen. ☑ Sie waren im Theater. ☐

Sie sind ins Kino gegangen. ☑

Sie sind zur Cutty Sark gegangen. ☑

Sie haben das Royal Oberservatory besucht. ☐

Sie haben einen berühmten Schauspieler getroffen. ☑

Wenn du ein wichtiges Wort nicht mehr weißt, kannst du es im Dictionary deines Schulbuchs ab Seite 196 nachschlagen.

○ **b)** Was ist richtig? Setze Haken.

1. Warum hat Jessie kein Buch gekauft?

   Es hat ihr keines gefallen. ☐

   Die Bücher waren zu teuer. ☑

2. Warum konnten sie nicht mit Daniel Radcliffe reden?

   Er war von zu vielen Menschen umringt. ☑

   Er stand zu weit oben auf der Bühne. ☐

Ziel 5: Ich kann touristische Informationen über Greenwich weitergeben.

○ **a)** Welche Sätze enthalten die gleiche Information? Verbinde sie.

1. Where can I find the Cutty Sark?
2. When can I go on the Cutty Sark?
3. Every day from ten to five o'clock.
4. How can I go to Greenwich?
5. There's the train, the underground and there are a lot of buses too.

a. Jeden Tag zwischen zehn Uhr morgens und fünf Uhr am Nachmittag.
b. Wo kann ich die Cutty Sark finden?
c. Man kann mit dem Zug, der U-Bahn oder dem Bus fahren.
d. Wie kann ich nach Greenwich fahren?
e. Wann kann ich auf die Cutty Sark gehen?

○ **b)** Sieh dir nun die Übung 5 auf Seite 65 noch einmal an. Kannst du sie jetzt lösen?

A trip to the country

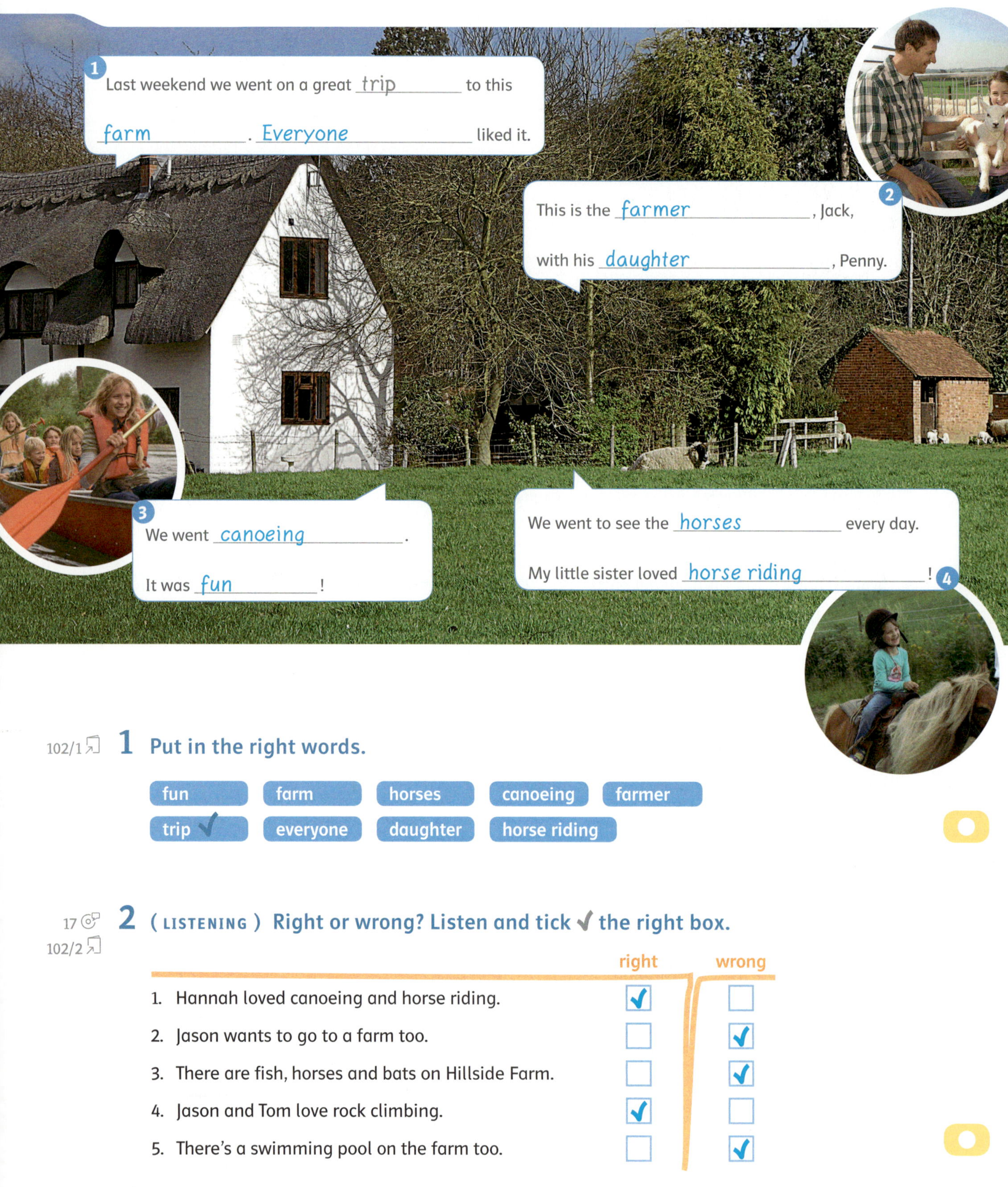

1 Last weekend we went on a great trip to this farm. Everyone liked it.
2 This is the farmer, Jack, with his daughter, Penny.
3 We went canoeing. It was fun!
4 We went to see the horses every day. My little sister loved horse riding!

102/1 **1 Put in the right words.**

fun · farm · horses · canoeing · farmer · trip ✓ · everyone · daughter · horse riding

17 102/2 **2 (LISTENING) Right or wrong? Listen and tick ✓ the right box.**

	right	wrong
1. Hannah loved canoeing and horse riding.	✓	
2. Jason wants to go to a farm too.		✓
3. There are fish, horses and bats on Hillside Farm.		✓
4. Jason and Tom love rock climbing.	✓	
5. There's a swimming pool on the farm too.		✓

1 man – 2 men
1 woman – 2 women

104/1

1 Cross out the wrong word.

1. horse riding ~~boring~~ canoeing rock climbing
2. men daughters women ~~sad~~
3. ~~accident~~ shoe pullover uniform
4. room garden attic ~~collar~~
5. skateboard bike ~~card~~ car

104/2

2 Find the words.

a) Match the words.

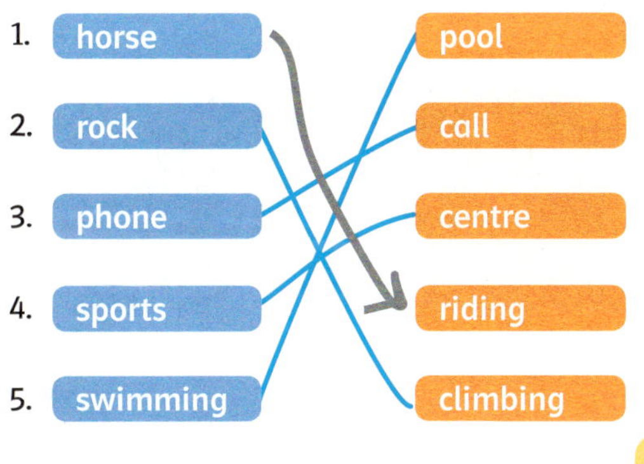

b) Write the words.

1. horse riding
2. rock climbing
3. phone call
4. sports centre
5. swimming pool

105/5

3 (SPEAKING) Make a phone call. Use the sentences or your own ideas. (Lösungsvorschlag)

See you soon! | I'm at home in my room. | Hello? ✓ | Sorry, it's time for lunch now. | I went rock climbing. It was great!

What did you do at the weekend? | OK. Bye. | Hi, is that you, . . . ? It's me, ... Where are you? | Cool, I'd also like to go rock climbing.

Partner A

Hello?

I'm at home in my room.

I went rock climbing. It was great!

Sorry. It's time for lunch now.

See you soon!

Partner B

Hi, is that you, ...? It's me, ...

Where are you?

What did you do at the weekend?

Cool, I'd also like to go rock climbing.

OK. Bye.

106/6 **4 Find the words.**

a) Find the words and write them.

fed, had, went, wore, saw, bought, did, was

b) Now write their simple present forms.

feed, have, go, wear, see, buy, do, is

106/7 **5 Look at the pictures and write what they did.**

1 go	2 go	3 have	4 wear
They went horse riding.	She went swimming.	They had a picnic.	He wore a helmet.

106/8 **6 Put in the right form of the verb.**

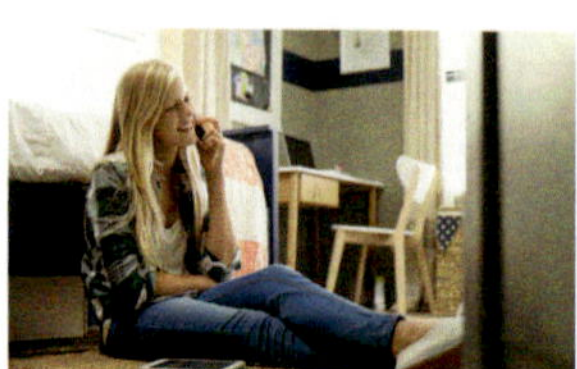

Hi, is that you, Aunt Sally? It's me, Hannah.

Hi Hannah! How are you?

Hannah: I'm fine, thanks.

Aunt Sally: How was ______ (be) your trip to the farm?

Hannah: We did ______ (do) a lot of great things! I had ______ (have) a picnic with Penny, the farmer's daughter, and we fed ______ (feed) the sheep. We also went ______ (go) horse riding. Mum wore ______ (wear) her special shoes. On Saturday night we went ______ (go) on a night walk. That was cool! Oh, and Dad bought ______ (buy) a pullover at the Hillside Farm shop. It's blue and has a horse on it. We really had ______ (have) a lot of fun! Would you like to come with us next time?

Aunt Sally: Yes, why not? Good idea, Hannah.

107/10 ## 7 Match the questions with the right answers.

1. Did Dad like it at the farm?
2. Did you feed the chickens?
3. Did Dad go horse riding?
4. Did he wear a helmet?
5. Did you buy some farm food?

a. Yes, we all did. No helmet – no horse riding. That's the rule.
b. No, we didn't. But you can buy many things: butter, bread, eggs.
c. No, we didn't. But we fed the sheep.
d. Yes, he did. He liked it a lot.
e. Yes, he did. And he wasn't scared of the horses.

107/11 ## 8 (SPEAKING) Talk about your weekend.

a) Complete the dialogue.

was | went | did | watched | is | see | are | go | had

Partner A	Partner B
Hello?	Hi, is ______ that you, …?
	It's me, ….
Hi …! How are ______ you?	
	I'm OK. Did ______ you have a nice weekend?
Yes, I did. I went ______ to the cinema.	
	Cool. How was ______ it?
It was awful. We watched ______ a boring film.	
	Oh no. And after that?
We had ______ pizza. That was great.	
	Good. Hey, let's go ______ to Tim's party next Saturday.
OK, great. Sorry, it's time for lunch.	
	OK. See ______ you soon!

b) Act the dialogue. You can also use the words or your own ideas. (Individuelle Lösung)

to a farm | Horse riding was boring. | Let's go canoeing. | …

Wo kannst du diese Wörter oder deine eigenen Ideen verwenden? Unterstreiche die Stellen zuerst im Text.

108/1 ## 1 Write the words.

1. coat
2. torch
3. mouse
4. tail

18
108/2 ## 2 (LISTENING) Hannah's postcard

a) Listen to Hannah's grandma. Which ten words do you hear? Put a circle ◯ around them.

(Dear)	Hi	(Yesterday)	on Sunday	homework	
(scary)	bad	(torch)	horse	(dark)	(rain)
(wet)	(coat)	(hamster)	said	mouse	
its	(tail)	longer	(best wishes)	teacher	

b) Listen again. Cross out the wrong words and correct them.

1. The night walk was ~~fun.~~ scary
2. Hannah had a ~~bag~~ with her. torch
3. It was ~~cold~~ and it rained. dark
4. That was ~~good~~ for Hannah and her friends. bad
5. Hannah wore her ~~pullover~~. coat
6. They all got ~~cold~~. wet
7. Hannah has a ~~mouse~~ now. hamster

torch
wet
scary ✓
hamster
bad
coat
dark

109/4 ## 3 (GAME) Play the game. (Individuelle Lösung)

Spielt zu zweit, zu dritt oder zu viert. Ihr braucht einen Würfel. Würfelt reihum und erfüllt die Aufgaben passend zu der Zahl, die ihr gewürfelt habt. Für jede richtig erfüllte Aufgabe gibt es einen Punkt. Der/Die Spieler/Spielerin mit den meisten Punkten nach drei Runden gewinnt.

Regelmäßige Verben sind z. B.: watch, like, play, help.
Unregelmäßige Verben sind z. B.: do, get, wear, feed, buy.

- ⚀ Nenne eine englische Vokabel, die du in dieser Unit gelernt hast.
- ⚁ Nenne ein unregelmäßiges englisches Verb und die simple past-Form dazu.
- ⚂ Sage einen englischen Satz über dein letztes Wochenende.
- ⚃ Nenne ein regelmäßiges englisches Verb und die simple past-Form dazu.
- ⚄ Sage einen englischen Satz über die Hillside Farm.
- ⚅ Joker! Du musst nichts tun!

• 4 Write sentences about what they didn't do on the farm yesterday.

110/7

feed / chickens | say / Woof! ✓ | eat / food
wear / helmet | like / horse

Sieh dir das Bild genau an und lies die Wörter darunter. Zu wem passen die Wörter im Bild? Bilde Sätze mit didn't.

1. The dog didn't say "Woof".
2. The farmer didn't feed the chickens.
3. The sheep didn't eat the food.
4. The cat didn't like the horse.
5. The girl didn't wear a helmet.

5 What didn't Ben do yesterday? (Lösungsvorschlag)

110/8

Write four sentences about what Ben didn't do yesterday.

go to bat school / ...	Yesterday Ben didn't go to bat school.
have lunch / breakfast / ...	He didn't have lunch in the cafeteria.
play football / netball / ...	He didn't play football in the playground.
do his homework	He didn't do his homework.
go to bed at 8:00 / ...	In the evening he didn't go to bed at 8:00.

Yesterday was Saturday and Ben went to a bat party.

6 Put in the right verbs.

111/9a

was | wasn't | saw | didn't see | came
started | didn't wear | went ✓ | got

Dear Olivia,

Last night Frank Turner, Jay and I _went_ on a night walk again, this time to an old tree house. Jay was on the ladder and he _saw_ some bats. He _was_ so happy. But then it got very dark so I _didn't see_ a bat. After that it _started_ to rain. This time I _got_ very wet because I _didn't wear_ a coat. We _came_ back to the farm at eleven, cold, wet and tired. That night walk _wasn't_ fun!

See you soon, Dave

7 (LISTENING) What did Mrs Turner say? Cross out the wrong words.

19
111/9

1. The class from London went ~~rock climbing~~ / canoeing.
2. It rained all day so they watched a DVD about ~~farm animals~~ / rock climbing.
3. After a night walk ~~a girl~~ / a boy didn't come back to the farm.
4. They all went out with torches / ~~GPS collars~~.
5. Barry, the farmer's dog, saw the boy behind the ~~tractor~~ / farm.
6. The boy wanted to feed the rabbits / ~~chickens~~.

8 Complete the postcard. (Individuelle Lösung)

111/10

great | exciting
boring | ...
Monday | ...
went canoeing / ...
played cards / ...
had a party / ...
didn't see ... / go ...
didn't play ... / have ...

Hi ________,

My trip is ________.

On ________ we ________.

Yesterday we ________,

but we ________.

See you next week, ________

112/2 **1** Complete the crossword.

What's the new word? Can you draw it? (Individuelle Lösung)

113/4 **2** (READING) Look at the pictures.

a) Read the story in your book on pages 112 and 113 again.
Find three mistakes in each picture.

Lösung: wheelchair, laptop, Dave and Holly

Mo-oo!

Lösung: sweatshirt, mud, Baa!

b) Now compare the mistakes with your partner. Did you find everything?

114/1 **3** (MEDIATION) Hilf einem Touristen die Schilder zu verstehen. (Lösungsvorschlag)

Don't go swimming in the river!
Don't have a picnic here!

FARM PARK
• Please do not play with our sheep.
• Do not feed the chickens!

WELCOME TO HILLSIDE FARM SHOP
Fresh eggs and cheese.
We also sell bread, butter, ham and meat.

1. Darf man hier schwimmen oder ein Picknick machen? Beides ist leider hier nicht erlaubt.
2. Was ist mit den Tieren? Man soll nicht mit den Schafen spielen oder die Hühner füttern.
3. Was ist das für ein Laden und was kann man da kaufen? Ein Bauernladen. Man kann hier frische Eier, Käse, Brot, Butter, Schinken und Fleisch kaufen.

Lösungen online as3kb5

___ /6P Ziel 1: Ich kann sagen, ob mir ein Ausflugsziel gefällt.

→p.78/1

Would you like to go to these places? Say why or why not. (Lösungsvorschlag)

1. Hillside Farm ✓ | animals | sports | the country | go horse riding | go canoeing | feed the sheep | fun | interesting | great
2. to the river | on a night walk | cold water | bats | awful | scary

1. I'd like to go to Hillside Farm because I like animals.

   You can go horse riding there. That's fun.

2. I wouldn't like to go to the river because I don't like cold water.

   It's / They're awful.

___ /6P Ziel 2: Ich kann ein Telefongespräch führen.

→p.78/2

You are at Hillside Farm. Complete this phone call with your mum.

Hi ✓ | Bye | Hello | great | I'm OK | went horse riding | it's time for

You: Hi ______ Mum. It's me, ______ (*name*).

Mum: Hello ______ (*name*). How are you?

You: I'm OK. Guess what! I went horse riding ______ yesterday. It was great.

Oh sorry, it's time for lunch.

Mum: OK. Bye.

___ /6P Ziel 3: Ich kann eine Postkarte schreiben. (Lösungsvorschlag)

→p.78/3

Write a postcard.

Hi | Dear | great | boring | OK | fun | ... | went rock climbing / canoeing / horse riding / on a night walk | helped the farmer with the animals | ... | soon | next week | on Monday | ...

Dear ______ (*name*),

Hillside Farm is great.

On Friday I went rock climbing.

Yesterday I helped the farmer with the animals.

See you next week,

______ (*your name*)

___/7P

Ziel 4: Ich kann eine Geschichte über einen Bauernhof verstehen.

→ p. 79/4

Lilly and Julia were at Hillside Farm. It was the last evening of their school trip. At ten o'clock all the students went to bed. But Lilly and Julia didn't. "Let's do something exciting!" said Julia. "Let's go on a night walk!" "We did that with Mrs Cole on Monday," said Lilly. "That was boring," said Julia. "It wasn't scary. Let's go on a night walk again – you and me!" "Oh OK," said Lilly, "but don't make a noise!" "It's cold and dark!" Lilly said. Suddenly there was a noise, "Baa, baa …" "Listen, there are sheep here." said Julia. "I don't like sheep." said Lilly. "Let's go to the farm." "Sheep aren't scary," Julia said. "They're nice! Let's find them. Do you have a torch?" Suddenly a sheep pushed Julia and she fell. "Where are you, Lilly? Help me, please. I'm stuck in the mud." "So sheep aren't always nice, are they?" Lilly said. "Would you like to go to the farm *now*?"

a) Read the text. Right or wrong? Tick ✓ the right box.

	right	wrong
1. The two girls went on a school trip to a farm.	✓	
2. Julia and Lilly went on a night walk again.	✓	
3. There was the noise of horses.		✓
4. A sheep pushed Lilly.		✓
5. Julia fell and got stuck in the mud.	✓	

b) Correct the wrong sentences.

There was the noise of sheep.

A sheep pushed Julia.

___/4P

Ziel 5: Ich kann Informationen von Schildern auf dem Land weitergeben.

→ p. 79/5

Beantworte die Fragen in Stichworten.

WELCOME TO HILLSIDE FARM!

Our activities for you:
- Go horse riding, rock climbing or canoeing.
- Help with the animals.
- Feed the chickens.

No dogs, please.

TICKETS
Adults £7.90
Children £2.10

OPENING TIMES
Farm 10:30–17:00
Shop 10:00–18:00

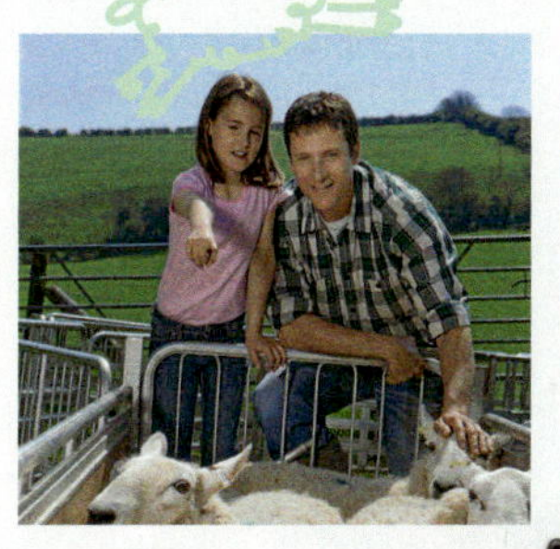

1. Was kann man auf der Hillside Farm tun?

   reiten, klettern, Kanu fahren, mit den Tieren helfen, Hühner füttern

2. Darf man seinen Hund mitbringen?

   Nein, das ist nicht erlaubt.

3. Was kostet der Eintritt für dich? £2.10

4. Wann ist der Laden geöffnet?

   von zehn bis sechs Uhr

Lösungen online as3kb5

Ziel 1: Ich kann sagen, ob mir ein Ausflugsziel gefällt.

○ a) Schreibe die Dinge, die etwas Schönes beschreiben, in die ☺-Spalte.
Schreibe die Dinge, die etwas Unangenehmes beschreiben, in die ☹-Spalte.

dirty | great | scary | sad | interesting ✓ | nice | boring | good | cool | awful

Listen wie diese helfen dir, Wörter zu ordnen. So kannst du sie dir besser merken.

☺	☹
interesting	scary
great	boring
nice	awful
cool	sad
good	dirty

○ b) Schreibe einen Satz über etwas Schönes und einen über etwas Unangenehmes. (Individuelle Lösung)

☺ ______ was ______.

☹ ______ was ______.

○ Ziel 2: Ich kann ein Telefongespräch führen.

Was sagst du beim Telefonieren? Setze einen Haken in das richtige Kästchen.

1. Du nimmst das Gespräch an.
   a) It's me. ☐
   b) Hello. ☑
2. Du willst wissen, wie es dem anderen geht.
   a) I'm OK. ☐
   b) How are you? ☑
3. Du willst erzählen, dass es dir gut geht.
   a) I'm OK. ☑
   b) The trip is OK. ☐
4. Du verabschiedest dich am Telefon.
   a) How was it? ☐
   b) See you soon. Bye! ☑

○ Ziel 3: Ich kann eine Postkarte schreiben. (Lösungsvorschlag)

Schreibe Lukes Postkarte an seinen Bruder Jamie. Wähle passende Wörter.

1. nice | cool | fun
2. fed the rabbits | went horse riding | had a picnic
3. feed the chickens | go canoeing | go horse riding
4. soon | on Sunday | next week

Dear Jamie,

It's cool (1.) here. Yesterday we fed the rabbits (2.).

I didn't feed the chickens (3.).

See you soon (4.),

Luke

Ziel 4: Ich kann eine Geschichte über einen Bauernhof verstehen.

Lilly and Julia were at Hillside Farm. They were on a school trip. At ten o'clock all the students went to bed. But Lilly and Julia didn't.
"Let's go on a night walk – you and me!" said Julia.
"Oh OK," said Lilly.

"It's cold and dark!" Lilly said.
Suddenly there was a noise, "Baa, baa …"
"There are sheep here." said Julia.
"I don't like sheep," said Lilly. "Let's go to the farm."
"No, Lilly, sheep are nice!" Julia said.

But then a sheep pushed Julia. She fell.
"Lilly! Help me! I'm here in the mud!"
"See, sheep aren't always nice, Julia," Lilly said. "Would you like to go to the farm *now*?"

○ **a)** Lies dir die Geschichte durch. Wer kommt in dieser Geschichte vor? Setze Haken.

 ☑
 ☐
 ☑
 ☐
 ☑
 ☐

○ **b)** Bringe die Sätze in die richtige Reihenfolge.

Auf der Hillside Farm liegen alle um zehn Uhr im Bett. 1

Dann wird Julia geschubst, so dass auch sie zurück zur Farm möchte. 6

Als sie draußen sind, hören sie ein Schaf blöken. 3

Lilly und Julia beschließen, eine Nachwanderung zu machen. 2

Julia findet aber, dass Schafe lieb sind, und möchte bleiben. 5

Lilly mag keine Schafe und möchte zurück zur Farm gehen. 4

○ **c)** Warum möchte Julia zum Schluss zurück zur Farm gehen? Setze einen Haken.

Sie wurde gebissen. ☐ Sie hat Angst und ihr ist kalt. ☐ Sie ist in den Matsch gefallen. ☑

○ Ziel 5: Ich kann Informationen von Schildern auf dem Land weitergeben.

Schau dir dieses Schild an und setze Haken an die richtigen Antworten.

WELCOME TO HILLSIDE FARM!
Here you can: (1.)
- Go horse riding.
- Help with the animals.
- Feed the chickens.

No dogs, please. (2.)

TICKETS
Adults £7.90
Children £2.10 (3.)

1. Was kann man hier tun? Setze drei Haken.

   Fahrrad fahren ☐ Reiten ☑

   Bei den Tieren helfen ☑

   Schwimmen ☐ Hühner Füttern ☑

2. Welches Schild passt?

    ☑  ☐  ☐

3. Wie viel Eintritt zahlt ein Kind?

   £7.90 ☐ £2.10 ☑ £1.20 ☐

Inhaltsverzeichnis der CD zum Hörverstehen
Hörverstehenstexte aus dem Workbook

Zusätzlich auf dieser CD:
- Alle Tracks des Workbooks als MP3-Dateien
- Lesetexte des Schülerbuchs als MP3-Dateien